Garden City

Anna Yudina

Garden City

Supergreen Buildings, Urban Skyscapes and the New Planted Space

With 308 illustrations

Thames & Hudson

First published in the United Kingdom in 2017 by
Thames & Hudson Ltd, 181A High Holborn,
London WC1V 7QX

*Garden City: Supergreen Buildings, Urban
Skyscapes and the New Planted Space*
© 2017 Anna Yudina
Illustrations © 2017 the copyright holders;
see page 256 for details

Designed by Anna Yudina

British Library Cataloguing-in-Publication Data
A catalogue record for this book is available from
the British Library

ISBN 978-0-500-34326-5

Printed and bound in China by C&C Offset
Printing Co. Ltd

To find out about all our publications, please visit
www.thamesandhudson.com. There you can
subscribe to our e-newsletter, browse or download our
current catalogue, and buy any titles that are in print.

Contents

Introduction

If the title *Garden City* sends your thoughts towards the green-belt towns associated with the garden city movement of 1890s Britain, make a U-turn. Inventor, futurist and Google's director of engineering Ray Kurzweil's prediction about 'the hybrid of biological and non-biological thinking' as a distinguishing trait of our not-so-distant future is the correct road sign here. So, head straight for the Big City. And then think of gardeners.

When Coloco, a team of progressive landscape architects, explain how they take their cues from the gardener as someone who respectfully observes the existing dynamics of nature and harvests its energies while trying to interfere with the natural processes as little as possible, I find that my interest has been piqued. When 'the gardener' emerges as one of the key themes in a conversation with Marco Casagrande, an architect whose work borders on environmental art and is largely inspired by guerilla urbanism, I listen carefully because our topic is the 'bio-urban city' that lives 'in tune with the life-providing systems of nature'. And when Luis Bettencourt, a theoretical physicist and expert in complex systems, currently involved in developing a mathematical theory of the city, brings up the gardener's attitude as the most relevant and life-friendly approach to city-making, the new meaning of the garden city starts to take shape

The garden city is a unique organism in which the natural and the man-made, construction and cultivation, the 'bio' and the 'digital', form one living and breathing whole. Just like any other garden, it is a combination of the designed and the spontaneous, while those who participate in city-making take on the role of a gardener who, rather than design a machine, has to enable a complex, ever-changing 'ecosystem'.

Humans have invented cities, and built transportation, utility and communications networks. We have been through two industrial revolutions and are now entering a third, based on global connectivity and the decentralized generation of renewable energy. Along the way we have become progressively disconnected from nature, and yet, by definition, have never ceased to be part of it. Today, we recognize the urgency of re-establishing this connection. The challenge is to not fall into the trap of superficial 'greening', but to connect in earnest – without, however, losing the advantages of living in the contemporary city.

In addition to other benefits, the presence of nature acts as a powerful fuel for our creative thinking – and therefore for our continued evolution. At the same time, the essence of the city consists in maximizing interactions between people in order to generate new ideas, products, activities and values. Imagine what a breeding ground for innovation will be the city that – in the words of Peter Cook, co-founder of the radical architectural collective Archigram – pulls 'the vegetal towards the artificial and the fertile towards the urban'.

Garden City looks at new design solutions, architectural forms and spatial practices that result from architects and urban designers making nature's intelligence, beauty and generosity their ally. A selection of built and ongoing projects, as well as a number of conceptual designs (many of them backed up by feasibility studies), highlights various facets of this immense topic.

What will it be like, functionally as well as aesthetically, if vegetation gets, once again quoting Peter Cook, 'knitted into the very substance of a building'? What can be done about the skyscraper, which is the most un-ecological building type, but which, at least for now, cannot be banned from our cities with their continuously growing populations? What are the design challenges for 'productive buildings' – for instance, the ones that will house industrial-scale urban farms or operate as building-sized air purifiers? Can concrete be growth-friendly? In densely built areas with no space for traditional parks, what are the alternative locations for nature, and how will these alter our experience of a park? Having already conquered urban façades and rooftops, where shall greenery go next? Can it become mobile? We may recall the floating park that cruised around Manhattan on a barge – an idea proposed by land-art pioneer Robert Smithson in 1970 and realized by the Whitney Museum of American Art with landscape designers Balmori Associates in 2005 – and why not imagine other, previously unthinkable kinds of mobility?

Some designers have created urban reserves that humans can admire but not enter, like Alan Sonfist's Time Landscape in New York or Gilles Clément's L'île Derborence in Lilles, France, a small forest perched on a 7-metre-high (23 feet) plinth. Others have encouraged urbanites to share their homes and offices with plant life, as in the 'biospheres' that form part of Amazon's new headquarters in Seattle, Washington, and which require a finely tuned balance of temperature and humidity to be fit for plants, people and laptops. Some designers have approached vegetation as a building material that should need as little maintenance as possible. Others have treated plants as the residents' companions – the living beings one finds pleasure in taking care of. Still others have developed hybrid designs in which biological organisms and digital technologies cooperate within a single system; envisioned architecture as an interface between people and nature; and conceived of buildings that incorporate change – the quality inherent to natural processes – as part of the design agenda.

How far can we expand the concept of 'urban nature'? How would it make us feel? And how is it going to transform our cities – and, eventually, ourselves? Some of the answers can be found in the pages that follow; others, gained from experience, in the years to come.

Fusion

Fusion

In this first chapter, we focus on those projects where the architects' responses to diverse factors – bleak surroundings, air pollution, local climate-related challenges – as well as the desire to reduce a project's energy footprint and otherwise increase its user value, bring in plant life as a critical element of the solution.

Luciano Pia's design for 25 Green, a residential block in Turin, Italy (page 15), incorporates trees – some of them up to 8 metres (26¼ feet) tall – to make a healing difference in a nondescript, formerly industrial area of a city with one of Europe's highest air-pollution levels. In the Mountain project in Copenhagen, Denmark (page 34), planted terraces are the result of Bjarke Ingels's quest to combine the advantages of urban high-rise living with those of a rural cottage within a single, coherent architectural solution. Studio Penda uses plant boxes as multipurpose elements in an assembly kit for a customizable apartment tower in Vijayawada, India (page 38), while the planted shading shelves on Jean Nouvel and PTW Architects' One Central Park tower in Sydney, Australia (page 22), are likely to outperform the more conventional metallic louvres. Pascale Dalix and Frédéric Chartier developed building blocks for a plant-, bird- and insect-friendly 'living façade' with countless nooks and crannies (page 48) – a possible reply to design scientist Melissa Sperry's concerns about 'the predominant architectural building materials being so truly obnoxious unto life as to prove uninhabitable even to that most hardy of species, lichen!' (from an essay for the Festival of the Future City, Bristol, UK, 2015).

In most of the buildings featured in this chapter, vegetation is also instrumental as a means of climate control. In fact, Édouard François went so far as to advise the residents of his Building that Grows in the southern French city of Montpellier (page 46) not to install air conditioners in their apartments.

Sometimes, says Vietnamese architect Vo Trong Nghia, one just asks, 'How many trees can we give back to the earth while designing a building?' Headquartered in a hot, polluted and humid megacity that desperately lacks vegetation, Nghia makes sure that his own projects come complete with an answer to this question. Moreover, his designs are both budget-savvy and scalable. Thus, Nghia's single-family House for Trees (page 18) – a group of structures that double as tree pots – served as a prototype for a larger scheme for the EPT University in Hoa Lac, Vietnam, in which multiple staggered 'tree-pot modules' form an iconic Gateway Building with accessible nature on every floor, but also enable shading and passive cooling. On a similar, if more luxurious, note, Singaporean office WOHA proves that the amount of greenery in a built-up city centre can not only be maintained but also increased. The lush, self-sustaining 'sky garden' of their Parkroyal on Pickering project in Singapore covers 15,000 square metres (161,459 square feet), twice the size of the building's footprint.

For plants to be able to thrive in environments in which they are not usually found, a fair amount of experimentation (which may eventually lead to industrial solutions) is required. This is especially true for designs that treat an architectural object like an element of the landscape – a half natural, half artificial 'landform'. Thus, Thomas Corbasson and Karine Chartier collaborated with an engineering company to develop a supporting structure for an irregularly shaped green façade that transformed their building into an extension of the adjacent park (page 50). Custom-designed for a particular project, the resulting low-tech, low-maintenance system can be used for other buildings as well. For the Torque House in Gyeonggi-do, South Korea (page 54), Mass Studies and their landscaping consultants tested the geotextile-based Moss Catch System as the façade-finishing material, while artistic projects by Heather Ackroyd and Dan Harvey (page 61) served as a catalyst for scientific research into the development of drought-tolerant plant species.

Speaking about 25 Green, Luciano Pia poetically described his intention behind the design as wishing to import a fragment of a river and a park. Yet the distinguishing feature of each of the projects in this chapter is that – rather than simply adding greenery to buildings – they hint at the possibility of new, different, hybrid forms of both architecture and nature.

White Walls – Tower 25

Jean Nouvel with Takis Sophocleous Architects / Nicosia, Cyprus

Jean Nouvel has said that he sees every project as an opportunity not only to add 'the missing pieces of the puzzle', but also to offer the most poetic and natural response to the context and the brief. Nouvel's white-walled, 66-metre-high (216½ feet) Tower 25 – the tallest building in the Cypriot capital and a new landmark for one the city's most significant locations, Eleftheria Square – appears to have been taken over by vegetation. Plants burst through the random-looking, pixelated perforation on the tower's east and west façades,

and overflow the deep, full-length, south-facing balconies. The vegetation – in fact, a selection of Cypriot climbing and spreading species – is said to cover nearly 80 per cent of the façade area, where they act as a natural sunshade and cooling device during Nicosia's hot and dry summers. Expect an interesting visual dialogue with the mathematics-meets-organic landscaping patterns of the new park, designed by Zaha Hadid as part of the major redevelopment of the square.

25 Green

Luciano Pia / Turin, Italy

Turin-based architect Luciano Pia describes 25 Green – a five-storey apartment building located in a former industrial zone – as a child's dream of a tree house coming true. The project's nondescript surroundings prompted Pia to consider an introverted scheme that would be like an oasis for its residents, while its proximity to the River Po and Valentino Park gave him the idea of 'importing' a fragment of both the river and the park into the new urban block.

The apartments were designed as irregularly stacked, empty modules of various shapes and sizes, giving their owners complete freedom to organize the interiors according to their needs and preferences. These residential modules are immersed in a 'habitable forest': each apartment has a large terrace planted with trees and shrubs, making a total of 140 trees for 63 units. An additional forty trees populate the courtyard garden. The resulting vertical forest is inseparable from the building: in the architect's words, cutting down one of these trees would be equal to demolishing a part of the structure.

Planters in cor-ten
steel, the diameters of
which vary from 2.3 to
4 metres (7½ to 13 feet),
are integrated into the
façade structure. They
house a large variety of
tree species, which range
in height from 2.5 to
8 metres (8 to 26 feet).

The plants form a 'soft', vibrant,
ever-changing protective screen that works
on both psychological and functional levels.
While large windows and external stairways
enhance the sense of continuity between
the inside and the outside, the abundant
foliage creates a filter between the living
spaces and the noisy street. It also acts as
a powerful air purifier – no small deal in
a city like Turin, where the air-pollution levels
are dangerously high. The use of deciduous
species provides shade and reduces heat
in the summer, but lets in more light during
the winter, when the trees lose their leaves.
The vegetation is irrigated with water from
a rainwater harvesting system.

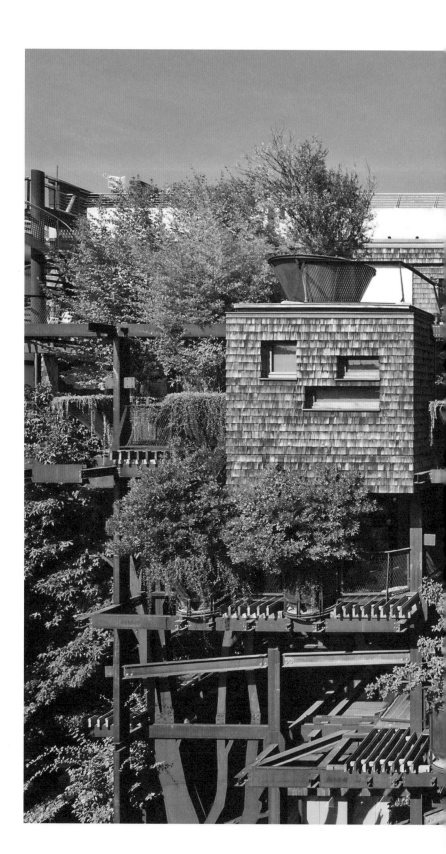

House for Trees

Vo Trong Nghia Architects / **Ho Chi Minh City, Vietnam**

While House for Trees is the name of just one project by Vo Trong Nghia, designing 'houses for trees' is nothing less than this Vietnamese architect's credo.

Nghia's main office is located in Ho Chi Minh City, known to have the least amount of green space of all the East Asian megacities: a mere 0.7 square metres (7½ square feet) per person (the average for such cities is 66.2 square metres/712½ square feet). Nghia aims to return nature to a city that suffers from pollution, frequent flooding and excessive heat.

Designed for a family of five, House for Trees was intended as a low-cost prototype dwelling with integrated tropical trees for the provision of shade and natural air conditioning. Requiring very little maintenance, the trees were also intended to make a positive contribution to the community.

Located in the city's most densely populated area and surrounded on all sides by tightly packed buildings, the house is split into five concrete volumes of various heights that double as giant tree pots. Containing a layer of soil 1.5 metres (5 feet) thick, they make space for a small rooftop park and double as stormwater detention tanks. (Permeable paving made of turf blocks is equally well adapted to draining rainwater.) If Nghia manages to turn his scheme into a serial design, it will help not only to reconnect his fellow citizens to nature, but also to reduce the risk of flooding.

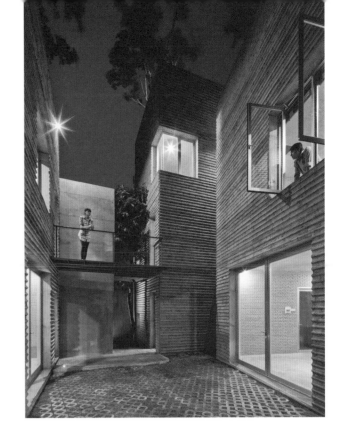

Built on a budget of US$156,000, the house consists of four connected volumes with a series of shared spaces on the ground floor – a library, a bathroom, a dining room and a kitchen – and bedrooms on the upper level. The free-standing fifth volume hosts a meditation space. All of this is topped with a 'hanging forest' that rests on a robust concrete structure. 'A tree is the cheapest sunshading device in Vietnam,' says Nghia, who used a local species costing just US$200 per tree.

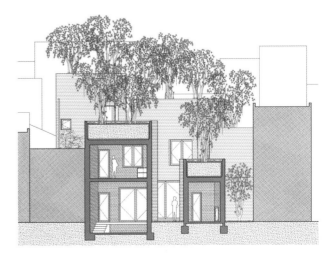

One Central Park

Jean Nouvel with PTW Architects / Sydney, Australia

Spinning off the main building at a height of 100 metres (328 feet), a monumental cantilever accommodates a sky garden, provides sun protection, and supports a uniquely sized, motorized heliostat. Guided by sun-tracking software, the heliostat's complex set of mirrors – partly hidden, partly visible – redirects sunlight being reflected off the roof of the smaller tower into the area that lies in the main building's shadow. Passers-by enjoy the dappled light that evokes a stroll under a green canopy.

'For me, vegetation is part of the vocabulary of architecture.' So said Jean Nouvel in relation to One Central Park, the first project to be built in the new development zone that marks the transition between the dense fabric of Sydney's central business district and the lower-rise residential suburb of Chippendale. Deployed on a former industrial site, the urban renewal scheme has a small neighbourhood park at its centre. Nouvel's design magnifies the scale of the park by covering 50 per cent of the façades of the 116- and 64.5-metre (380½- and 212-foot) residential towers with more than 35,000 plants – to 'extend the park into the sky' and eventually set the record for the world's tallest vegetated wall to date.

Enormous green panels were made possible by French botanist Patrick Blanc's vertical-garden technology, in which the roots of plants grow into layers of polyamide felt soaked in a nutrient solution. Still other vegetation populates a system of horizontal planters 5 kilometres (3 miles) long. These planters act as permanent shading shelves and, according to the journal of the Council on Tall Buildings and Urban Habitat, reduce the thermal impact in the apartments by about 20 per cent, while the plant foliage diminishes heat gains by an additional 20 per cent. Compared to metallic louvres, plants offer yet further advantages, trading carbon dioxide for oxygen and reflecting less heat back into the city.

Waterloo Youth Centre

Collins and Turner / Sydney, Australia

Weave, a non-profit organization serving disadvantaged young people, has been headquartered in a former amenities block with a view over a skate park for more than a decade. Sydney-based architectural firm Collins and Turner, led by Penny Collins and Huw Turner, has converted the structure into a contemporary workplace.

Intended as a robust and long-lasting scheme with a low environmental impact, the renovated Waterloo Youth Centre maintains and reuses, wherever possible, elements of the existing structure.

The project's angular form recalls both origami and stealth aircraft. Other sources of inspiration, according to the architects, included 'the grass-covered Iron Age forts of Celtic Wales; the aviary at London Zoo designed by Cedric Price; and the work of John Krubsack – an American naturalist who experimented with growing and grafting plants into shapes, creating the first chair that was grown rather than made.'

Perhaps the project's most striking feature is the star-shaped steel canopy, which not only veils a roof garden but also supports a variety of climbing and fruit-producing plants. To reduce the building's apparent size, the design team partially embedded it in the ground by means of a series of subtle adjustments in the level of the landscape. As plants begin to overgrow the canopy and exterior metal grille, Collins and Turner expect the structure to merge gradually with the surrounding park and 'become an abstract and sculptural green landform'.

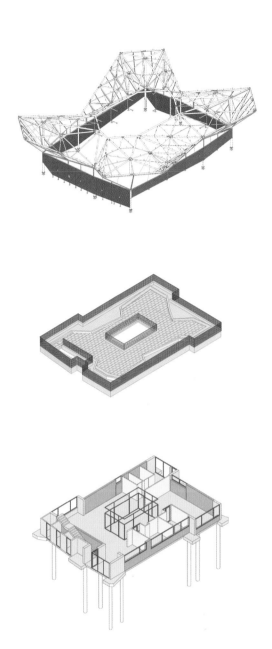

Robust galvanized steel is utilized for the building's distinctly urban exterior design, evoking such familiar details of inner-city life as railings, crash barriers, shutters and gratings. Concealed behind the faceted concrete and steel façades is a light-filled, flexible and functional interior based around a new central courtyard and crowned with a self-supporting, easy-to-dismount steel canopy.

House K

Sou Fujimoto / Nishinomiya, Japan

A new form of garden was imagined by Sou Fujimoto for this family house in a quiet residential suburb. The architect has revisited the large roof, a prominent element in traditional Japanese architecture, to turn it into an 'active living area' complete with a garden. In House K, the roof is treated as both an organic extension of the interior and an aspect of the landscape. Like a hillside, it slowly rises from the ground up, while at the same time giving shape to the living spaces below. The building's north façade makes a steep tilt, and trees in faceted, deliberately exposed pots seem to float above the roof.

The sloping surface, which is simultaneously a roof and a wall, rises from a neighbourhood grove to the height of 76.7 metres (252 feet), opening views towards the wooded hills to the west of the area. The residents' immediate surroundings, the intimacy of the domestic interior, the skyline and the distant landscape are all tied together in a single, rich experience.

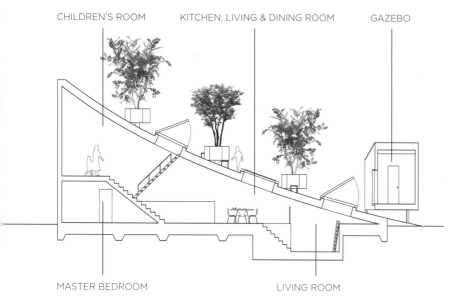

CHILDREN'S ROOM   KITCHEN, LIVING & DINING ROOM   GAZEBO

MASTER BEDROOM   LIVING ROOM

With House K, Fujimoto sought
to break away from what he describes
as 'normal' architecture, in which the
interior and the rooftop garden would
have been distinct from each other, and
create 'a more natural and geographical
relationship' between them. The project's
three-level interior topography includes
a kitchen, living and dining room; a loft
raised above the main level and reached
by a set of tiered stairs; and a sunken living
room on the other side of this open-plan,
softly lit home. Fujimoto's 'inside–outside'
circulation system uses ladders and operable
skylights to ensure that each level has its
own direct connection to the roof. One can
exit on to the roof from the loft, walk down
the sloped garden, and re-enter the house
from the other end.

A small gazebo sits at the lower end
of the roof. Together with a few pieces of
furniture anchored at different places across
the slope, it offers further opportunities to
enjoy this unusual garden.

Stone House

Vo Trong Nghia Architects / Dong Trieu, Vietnam

This torus-shaped design by Vo Trong Nghia both determines and is determined by the way the residents – a couple with two children – move about the place. Inside, four clusters of rooms are arranged around an oval courtyard. These clusters are separated by 'voids', providing spaces where the family can spend time together. In addition, these voids facilitate natural lighting and ventilation, and connect the external and courtyard gardens. The pool in the courtyard naturally cools the rooms.

A circulation path connects all parts of the house as it rounds the courtyard and continues to the green roof. The courtyard and the roof form a 'sequential garden' that allows the residents to experience the indoor and outdoor parts of their home in a fluid, natural and playful manner. At the same time, the rising spiral roof makes for different ceiling heights and varied use of the space below. Thus, the double-height living room has a ceiling almost 5 metres (16 feet) high, while two low-ceilinged bedrooms are stacked on top of each other.

The project celebrates such local materials as blue stone and hardwood. The walls are composed of stone blocks 10 centimetres (4 inches) thick; trapezoid-shaped stones laid in an alternating pattern form the building's curved parts. The resulting three-dimensional texture generates rich light-and-shadow effects.

The Mountain

BIG / Copenhagen, Denmark

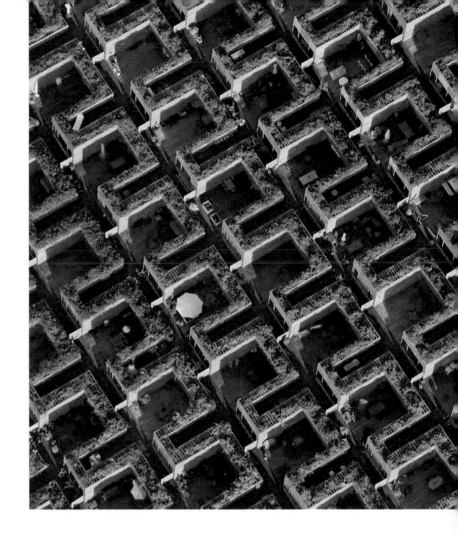

Strictly speaking, Bjarke Ingels's Mountain project is not specifically centred on nature. These terraced gardens came to life as a consequence of the Danish architect's 'alchemic' approach. Taking ingredients that, at first glance, might seem mutually exclusive, Ingels merges them into symbiotic schemes in which each programme finds its ideal place. This innovative mixture then creates added value for the project as a whole.

The Mountain was designed for a client who needed two separate buildings: a 10,000-square-metre (107,640-square-foot) condominium, and a 20,000-square-metre (215,280-square-foot) parking facility. The project is located in Ørestad City, Copenhagen's emerging district that borders a typical suburban neighbourhood.

To provide the double exposure required by Danish building regulations, the project's L-shaped courtyards allow for south- and west-facing windows. An underground cistern stores rainwater for the drip irrigation of the terraced gardens.

Uncompromising in his aim to create designs that will please everyone involved, Ingels follows the spirit rather than the letter of briefs and regulations. Instead of erecting, as he put it, 'a standard apartment slab next to a boring parking block', Ingels turned the parking facility into a sloped podium for the apartments. The surrealist outcome – defined by Ingels as a concrete hillside covered with a thin layer of housing that cascades from the eleventh to the first floor – combines the advantages of urban and suburban lifestyles. The Mountain maintains the density of a high-rise while offering each family a home with a garden, a penthouse view and a parking place on the same floor.

Tree Storey

Penda / Vijayawada, India

Responding to a commission from an innovation-friendly developer, design studio Penda came up with the idea of mass customization at an architectural scale. 'In an age of mass production and a certain conformism in the building industry,' explain the designers, 'we try to use modern construction techniques to bring back a degree of individualism and flexibility for the inhabitants of a high-rise. A kind of individualism one would have in building one's own house.'

The result is a residential tower designed as a modular system, in which the structural frame and infrastructure are the only fixed elements. Everything else is regarded as a plug-in to be slotted into the grid. The residents are invited to personalize their apartments by choosing all façade elements, flooring and plant boxes from a catalogue of prefabricated components.

The idea of a modular high-rise stemmed from an earlier project: a shelving system for a new Chinese café chain. In order to provide the chain with flexible interiors while treating customers to a breath of fresh air in pollution-plagued cities, Penda devised a slender framework to be filled with different items, including air-purifying plants. The Vijayawada project, too, puts greenery into focus – hoping that, over time, plants will grow into a key design element, with the architecture humbly stepping into the background.

In the Tree Storey project, 'vegetal modules' play multiple roles. In addition to forming partitions and exterior privacy screens for largely open-plan residences, they provide natural sunshading and purify the air – especially the plants used on the façade, for which the designers recommend species with high pollutant-absorbing capacities.

Hualien Residences

BIG / Hualien, Taiwan

A former industrial region on the east coast of Taiwan is being transformed into a tourist destination. While the developer is planning to accompany this next-generation beach resort with equally advanced facilities for the 'Huallywood' film studios currently under construction, BIG architects – commissioned to design the Hualien Residences – have reaffirmed their capacity to 'turn surreal dreams into inhabitable space'. Located some 5 kilometres (3 miles) from Hualien City, the scheme takes its cues from the surrounding landscape: a mountain range to the west and the coast to the east. Bjarke Ingels's team adopted 'a language of green landscape stripes' to design a 'mountainscape' of more than 600 holiday homes and a host of additional programmes, from shops to art venues.

The project's 'topographic' design will create a landscape of hills and valleys, with the stylized mountain shapes forming 'pedestrian canyons and shortcuts between the buildings'. Vertically sliced volumes boast full-height glazing, while the offset arrangement of these volumes ensures that every residence receives ample daylight. The orientation of the project makes the most of the available views and provides effective shading for the hot and humid climate. Planted roofs echo the wooded mountains and mitigate heat gain.

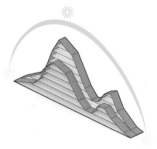

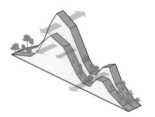

SUN ORIENTATION

PEDESTRIAN CIRCULATION

INTERNAL VIEWS

Stacking Green

Vo Trong Nghia Architects / Ho Chi Minh City, Vietnam

Built on a plot measuring 20 x 4 metres (66 x 13 feet), this home is typical of Ho Chi Minh City's long and narrow 'tube houses'. Less typical is the building's design – a form of architectural acupuncture intended to mitigate an aggressive environment in which new development has driven out greenery. Created by Vo Trong Nghia, the project gives architectural shape to the citizens' much-loved practice of surrounding themselves with vegetation and displaying it on their houses. 'Even in the modernized city,' Nghia comments, 'people unconsciously desire the substitute of rampant tropical forest.'

The façades at both front and rear are composed of planters acting as large horizontal louvres. These green façades protect against direct sunlight, noise and pollution; contribute to the residents' well-being; and ensure their privacy in a friendly, non-defensive manner. The combination of permeable façades, a courtyard and an open-plan layout – bioclimatic cues taken from traditional Vietnamese houses – allows for ample natural ventilation. Despite the harsh climate, the family needs very little air conditioning, which keeps the electricity bills for this four-storey, 215-square-metre (2,314-square-foot) house remarkably low.

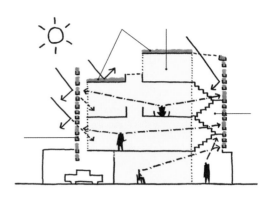

Cantilevered from the building's side walls, full-width planters form its front and rear façades. The gap between each planter was determined by the height of the plants, which varies from 25 to 40 centimetres (9⅞ to 15¾ inches). An automatic irrigation system feeds off a rainwater collection tank.

The Building that Grows

Édouard François with Duncan Lewis / Montpellier, France

At the heart of this residential project in Montpellier is a contemporary interpretation of the old Mediterranean gabion wall – notably, its potential for creating architecture with a 'living skin'. During construction of the project's walls, bags of organically fertilized potting soil carrying the seeds of various climbing plants were placed behind crushed stones; these, in turn, were contained within cages made of stainless-steel mesh.

More than a decade after its completion, the building continues to rely on passive climate control. 'It's probably the only upscale housing project in the entire city that does without air conditioning,' commented architect Édouard François. 'At the beginning, there were plans to install it, yet I persuaded the residents to wait for one year to see if it was necessary.' François knew that the self-watered plants growing out of the building's walls would do the job perfectly.

Biodiversity School

Chartier Dalix / **Boulogne-Billancourt, France**

Pascale Dalix and Frédéric Chartier treat buildings as complex architectural landscapes. Masterplanned as the green centrepiece of a new residential block, this scheme is no exception. A school and a gymnasium are packed into a single tiered structure. Surrounded by taller buildings, its roof is designed to enhance the neighbours' views. Three upper terraces host a meadow, a shrubbery and a small forest, and are fluidly connected to welcome human visitors and, no less importantly, to facilitate an 'ecological corridor'.

The project's most exciting feature, however, is its exterior envelope, known as 'the living wall'. The architects went to great lengths to make it plant-, bird- and insect-friendly – to the extent that all of these life forms are able to make it their home. This is achieved with the help of custom-designed concrete blocks that form all sorts of nooks and crannies in which birds can nest, plants can grow, and pipistrelle bats can roost. Grooves carved into some of the blocks channel off rainwater to keep the façade blemish-free.

Chamber of Commerce and Industry

Chartier-Corbasson Architectes / Amiens, France

Traditional green-wall schemes would
not have worked in this case because
they require a vertical surface.
Instead, the project uses a bespoke
façade system, in which standard
rectangular planters are mounted
on a superstructure made of metal
tubes and rails connected by specially
developed joints, which allow the
desired irregular shape to be created.

'As city and nature increasingly mix with each
other,' says architect Thomas Corbasson,
'it becomes exciting and even necessary to
artificialize nature and naturalize the city.'
Responding to a competition brief for the
renovation and extension of the Picardy
Regional Chamber of Commerce and
Industry in Amiens, France, his firm chose to
take a nearby park – and not the eighteenth-
century mansion that had previously housed
the Chamber – as its point of reference.
The new building's courtyard-facing façade
merges with the existing landscape and its
artificial rocks; large bay windows appear to
have been cut into the green mass.

     As the park already had its own
irrigation and water-management systems,
the green façade could simply be 'plugged'
into the circuit. The technical aspects of
covering the irregular, three-dimensional
façade with a continuous layer of vegetation
proved much trickier. Together with a group
of engineering consultants, the architects
developed a modular, low-tech solution.
Custom-designed for this project, their
system can be adapted for use with other
complex façade geometries.

Torque House

Mass Studies / Gyeonggi-do, South Korea

The upper part of this house for a family of four – designated as a 'linear' building in the local masterplan – is slightly slanted and curved in order to optimize the amount of daylight it receives. It also responds to the bend of the road in front of the main façade. 'As sharp stones are worn down by a flowing stream and transformed into pebbles, the rectangular building becomes torqued through the movement of curves,' says Minsuk Cho, principal architect at Mass Studies, the firm he founded in 2003. Challenged to design a residence incorporating two studios – one for a sound engineer and the other for his artist wife – Cho allowed the form and appearance of the façades to be largely determined by the different functions housed inside. The double-height artist's atelier on the ground floor, protected from outside distractions and lit only by a narrow strip of windows, and the soundproofed recording studio above contribute to the building's mostly introverted frontage. To balance this, it was decided to avoid 'excessively spartan' materials for exterior cladding. After much deliberation, a landscape designer suggested trying the Moss Catch System, a kind of geotextile originally intended, explains Cho, for improving the appearance of retaining walls. Gradually, a layer of moss has covered the Torque House's front and rear façades, reaffirming the idea of a building that blends into the landscape.

The Moss Catch System on the front and rear façades uses two types of mosses that adapt well to both north and south exposures. For the landscaping company that imported the technology from Japan, it was the first time it had been used as a finishing material. As such, they had to help the architects resolve a number of technical issues, such as the installation of watering facilities.

Ann Demeulemeester Store

Mass Studies / Seoul, South Korea

Carpeted by Japanese spurge, a herbaceous perennial planted in geotextile pockets, the building has a 40 x 40-centimetre (15¾ x 15¾-inch) grid of irrigation pipes installed throughout the front façade. A drainage gutter at its bottom edge captures excess water. The automated watering system is attuned to seasonal climate change, while the modular panels can be replaced individually, when necessary.

For a residential area that was rapidly evolving into a commercial district full of upscale boutiques and eateries, Minsuk Cho and his Seoul-based firm Mass Studies designed a building that had it all: a flagship store for Belgian fashion designer Ann Demeulemeester on the ground floor, a restaurant with a roof terrace above, and a multi-brand shop in the basement.

Driven by the idea of a high-end fashion store giving back to the community, Cho wished to incorporate in the project as much nature as would fit into a footprint of 378 square metres (4,069 square feet) on a site located in a low-rise, high-density neighbourhood. The architects teamed up with landscape experts from Garden in Forest and Vivaria Project to develop an indoor-meets-outdoor environment, in which natural and artificial elements would exist in 'amalgamation rather than confrontation'.

The building's front façade bends around a parking bay before jutting forward to highlight the entrance to the restaurant and the underground store. Except for the rounded windows, it is entirely covered with a carpet of plants. Years after its completion in 2007, the green façade remains intact.

A bamboo hedge marks the limits of the site on three other sides. The columns of the supporting structure in earth-coloured concrete blend into the organically shaped ceiling to form large arched openings that make the interior completely transparent.

The hedge acts as a screen, protecting the building from the street, yet also creates a sense of intimacy. Generous glazing renders the bamboo walls visible even from the road.

There is also another garden, buried 5.5 metres (18 feet) below ground level. What starts as a narrow white stairway leading downwards expands into a moss-covered cave, which has openings to the exterior that reinforce the indoor–outdoor nature of this synthetic architectural 'organism'.

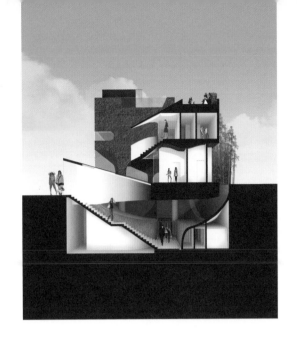

The Moss Catch System is used for the curved walls in the basement space, which has openings at both the front and the back to provide natural ventilation. Lighting and a mist-maker help to create a habitat suitable for the well-being of moss.

Flytower & Cunningham

Ackroyd & Harvey / London and Derry, UK

Grass grown from seed on vertical planes is the signature medium of British artists Heather Ackroyd and Dan Harvey, whose works explore the 'processes of germination, growth, erosion and decay'. Pressed into a hand-spread layer of soft clay, the seeds begin to sprout, transforming a wall or other vertical surface into a living skin of green grass. Some of Ackroyd & Harvey's works use grass as photographic paper. When exposed to different amounts of light, the blades of grass produce a larger or smaller concentration of chlorophyll. The resulting palette of greens and yellows closely replicates the shades of grey in a photographic image.

In another series, a 'mantle of grass' is grown on various buildings. In 2007 the concrete façades of the enormous and enigmatic flytower of the National Theatre – one of London's most familiar landmarks – turned green for an entire month (above and opposite, bottom). In 2013, at the invitation of Void gallery in Derry, Northern Ireland, the artists applied their technique to the Cunningham building at Ebrington (opposite, top, and overleaf), turning an abandoned military structure into a 'temporal and living' place.

Ackroyd & Harvey's work often overlaps with science. A collaboration with IGER (Institute of Grassland and Environmental Research) led to the development of the 'stay-green' strains of grass that have enabled the artists' photosynthesis-based works to last for years without fading. Their use of drought-resistant hybrids for the flytower at London's National Theatre represents more than just artistic curiosity, given the earth's increasingly unpredictable climate. For their part, the scientists at IGER say that some of their research would never have been undertaken without the questions raised by the artists.

Expansion

Expansion

While it is virtually impossible to create a genuine forest in an urban context, there are ways to create the *experience* of a forest. This is evocation rather than imitation, says American landscape architect Laurie Olin, the mastermind behind New York's overwhelmingly successful Bryant Park. Speaking in an interview with the Cultural Landscape Foundation, Olin goes on to describe one of his studio's projects: a parking garage in California with canyon-like gaps that provide natural ventilation and break the enormous structure into smaller parts. Planted in these gaps are redwood trees (whose natural habitat is moist, shady canyons), which provide the garage users with a rendezvous with nature.

Besides matching a local species of tree to the practical requirements of the project and thereby awakening the city-dweller's sense of wonder, this design is particularly fascinating for another reason. Namely, that the resulting direct encounter with nature – complete with views, smells and touch – happens in a place where it is least expected.

Today, urban centres leave little to no land for designing parks in a traditional way. As a consequence, architects and landscape specialists have to find less obvious solutions to the problem of creating new green spaces in an urban setting.

When officials in Madrid decided to redirect through a tunnel a riverfront section of the ring road that ran too close to the historic city centre, the use of the reclaimed area above the tunnel was decided by means of an international competition. As explained by urban and landscape architects West 8, the winning – and implemented – proposal they developed in conjunction with architectural firms Burgos & Garrido, Porras La Casta and Rubio & A-Sala was the only one that suggested 'resolving the urban situation exclusively by means of landscape architecture'. In Tainan, Taiwan, urban design and architectural studio MVRDV plans to replace a failed and unattractive shopping centre with a lush, green urban lagoon that will reconnect the city to its waterfront. In Washington, DC, a joint project by OLIN and OMA will transform an ageing road bridge in one of the city's most disadvantaged areas into an extraordinary civic space – a 'bridge park' with various kinds of activity zones, intended to function as a major recreational hub.

In a study produced for the think tank that develops strategies for the Greater Paris area, architects Louis Paillard and Philippe Gazeau, together with urban and landscape design agency TER, proposed a series of schemes for reclaiming the region's underused spaces – the retail parks and infrastructural fringes that add up to large amounts of potentially valuable land. One of these schemes involved clusters of living units raised on stilts above the islands of the River Seine as a means of populating these flood-prone areas. By leaving the ground unoccupied, the scheme would both protect the homes from flooding and enable the creation of new landscapes. The scheme's proposers identified thirty-five sites that could accommodate 150,000 residents plus '400 hectares [almost 1,000 acres] of biodiversity'. Another scheme focused on the urban potential of the 'islands' and fringes of land formed by intersecting railway lines. If properly reconnected to the city – inside which they are actually located – some 1,215 of these sites could be transformed into mixed-use neighbourhoods in which parks, gardens and community facilities would shield residential buildings placed at the core of the new landscapes.

In this chapter, we look at ways in which architecture and the landscaping professions have joined forces to develop new typologies, new practices and new means of experiencing both nature and the city. In some of the projects, plants have appropriated the vertical dimension. While Taketo Shimohigoshi has suspended a green artwork above the ground to give people in a cramped neighbourhood a reason to look out of their upper-floor windows (page 73), Stefano Boeri has planted trees on the balconies of a residential tower to create a modestly sized 'forest' in a densely built city (page 74); Édouard François, meanwhile, intends to place a stack of weekend cabins on top of another tower (page 78). Other designs reclaim abandoned infrastructural or industrial sites; examples range from a disused foundry to an elevated railway line, and, still more radically, from a submarine base to an underground trolley-car terminal.

Diaspora Garden

atelier le balto / Berlin, Germany

With a focus on the importance of education, the W. Michael Blumenthal Academy – the latest addition to the Jewish Museum Berlin – hosts the museum's library and archives, as well as spaces for seminars and workshops. In refurbishing a former flower market located across the street from the main building, the museum's architect, Daniel Libeskind, has built into the existing, hangar-like structure three tilted, wood-panelled cubes; housing the entrance, the lecture hall and the library, the cubes are designed to resemble transport crates and Noah's Ark. Further inside, visitors encounter an interior garden, in which two of the academy's main concerns – migration and diversity – are explored through a selection of plants. Interviewed in 2012 for the Berlin Biennale blog, Cilly Kugelmann, the museum's then programme director, commented that, after abandoning the initial idea of a biblical garden because the local climate was unfit for Middle Eastern plants, the museum 'turned to the idea of a Garden of Diaspora, looking at plants that are used for Jewish holiday rituals in Germany, fruits that substitute biblical offerings and even plants that were given anti-Semitic names'.

Landscape architects atelier le balto have arranged the garden on four steel 'plateaus', three of which host 'uprooted' planting beds. The fourth serves as a testing ground for new educational ideas, and features such diverse materials as maps, photos, soil, seeds and plant pots. Change, explain the designers, is fundamental to the project, in which 'plants can be seen in various stages of development,' while 'the variable beds allow for the emergence of new constellations and topics.'

Occupying 900 square metres (9,688 square feet), the Diaspora Garden is a landscape sculpture consisting of four steel 'plateaus', each measuring 4 x 14 metres (13 x 46 feet), that seem to float above a wooden deck. Set at oblique angles to one another and divided by a series of walkways, the plateaus form a pattern that echoes the expressive design language of the museum's architect, Daniel Libeskind. The plant beds are lit by energy-saving, daylight-simulating grow lamps.

FLEG Daikanyama

A.A.E. – Taketo Shimohigoshi / Tokyo, Japan

Although the local building code requires that apartment buildings have balconies, the occupants of this tightly packed residential area in the heart of Tokyo hardly use them. So observed architect Taketo Shimohigoshi as he explored the site on which a client had commissioned him to design a showroom topped with offices. While a variety of shops creates a lively atmosphere at street level, the upper parts of the buildings produce a cramped, charmless view that offers nothing to enjoy from one's balcony.

Shimohigoshi's project for FLEG Daikanyama makes a difference not only for its own residents but also for those of the neighbouring residential blocks. Two white walls close off unattractive lateral views and create a courtyard that opens towards an alley. Overhead, a series of beams connect the two walls. From below, the beams appear as a geometrical artwork in polished metal; when seen from the upper floors, they reveal velvety stripes of moss that turn bright green on rainy days. According to Shimohigoshi, a glimpse of vegetation suspended in mid-air within a dense urban site awakens the city-dweller's sensitivity to the power of life and stirs their imagination.

Vertical Forest

Boeri Studio / Milan, Italy

Stefano Boeri describes his Vertical Forest as 'biological architecture', an alternative to a 'strictly technological and mechanical approach to environmental sustainability'. Designed for Milan's up-and-coming Isola district – a former working-class neighbourhood cut off from the rest of the city by railway tracks – these two residential towers host enough trees, shrubs and ground-cover plants to fill a couple of hectares in a regular forest. In fact, Boeri considers the 'vertical densification of nature' as a way for Milan and other cities to solve the problem of insufficient ground-level space for green areas. Moreover, this model could be used to counter urban sprawl in the developing areas of heavily populated cities: according to Boeri, each Vertical Forest tower contains the equivalent of 50,000 square metres (538,200 square feet) of suburban one-family homes.

Milan's Vertical Forest consists of two towers, 80 and 112 metres (262½ and 367½ feet) high, which together host 480 large and medium-sized trees, 300 small trees, 11,000 perennial and covering plants, and 5,000 shrubs. In other words, Stefano Boeri's scheme fits the equivalent of 2 hectares (5 acres) of forest and undergrowth into some 1,500 square metres (16,150 square feet) of urban space.

It took three years to develop the garden system for Vertical Forest. The design team – which included Emanuela Borio and Laura Gatti, in charge of the vertical landscape design – collaborated with a group of botanists not only to select the plant species that would fit in the designated slots on the balconies, but also to devise their optimum distribution in relation to altitude and façade orientation. The trees, some of which should grow to a height of 9 metres (29½ feet), were tested in a wind turbine to make sure they would pose no danger if planted on the upper floors. The plants were pre-cultivated in a nursery, where they became accustomed to their future living conditions.

On average, Boeri's design provides two trees, eight shrubs and forty other plants per resident. In addition – to quote the architect himself – it 'promotes the formation of an urban ecosystem able to be inhabited by birds and insects'. With an initial estimate suggesting the eventual presence of some 1,600 specimens of birds and butterflies, hopes are that Vertical Forest will become a magnet for nature's recolonization of the city.

Green Cloud

Édouard François / Grenoble, France, and Gurgaon, India

In the Grenoble scheme (above), nicknamed 'Panache', every residence has its own roof terrace with a garden. Apartments that have a less favourable orientation are granted the terraces with the best configurations; those living on the lowest floors with north-facing windows will enjoy the topmost, south-looking terraces.

The brainchild of French architect Édouard François, the first Green Clouds, or multilevel rooftop extensions for urban homes, will make their debut on top of Gurgaon 71, a series of residential high-rises in Gurgaon, India. At a height of 125 metres (410 feet), where the climate becomes considerably fresher even without air conditioning, terraces with a capacity for growing trees will serve as weekend homes. Fitted with a kitchenette and a bathroom, they will be located just an elevator-ride away from the owner's main residence.

François has developed a similar scheme for an apartment tower in Grenoble, France (opposite), a city with cold winters and hot summers. In order to maintain comfortable interior temperatures throughout the year, the project does away with traditional balconies, using instead the architect's 'gardens in the attic', which provide the residents of the tower's modestly sized apartments with an additional 35 square metres (377 square feet) in which to relax, entertain guests and enjoy unobstructed views.

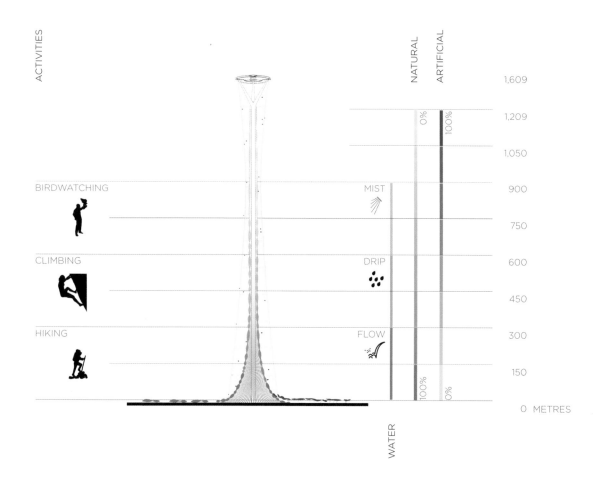

ACTIVITIES

NATURAL

ARTIFICIAL

1,609

0%

100%

1,209

1,050

BIRDWATCHING

MIST

900

750

CLIMBING

DRIP

600

450

HIKING

FLOW

300

150

100%

0%

0 METRES

WATER

Besides the augmented-reality experiences available in the Mile's circulation capsules, its vertical park will allow for a range of nature-related activities, such as hiking, climbing and birdwatching. Architect Carlo Ratti likens the Mile's green domain to New York's Central Park turned on its end, then rolled and twirled around the mile-high shaft.

The Mile

Carlo Ratti Associati, Schlaich Bergermann Partner, Atmos

About twice the height of today's tallest building, the Burj Khalifa, and taller than the under-construction, kilometre-high Jeddah Tower, the Mile was conceived as a 1,609-metre-tall (1 mile) vertical park topped with a constellation of 'sky decks' offering unprecedented views and thrilling high-altitude experiences. Multifunctional capsules fitted out for meetings, dinners and concerts will shuttle visitors to the top of the tower.

The concept was developed for an undisclosed client by Carlo Ratti Associati in collaboration with German engineers Schlaich Bergermann and British digital design studio Atmos. Although at the time it was not intended for any particular location, the project included advanced feasibility studies from both a financial and an engineering point of view. Notably, the structural solution was devised by the engineering firm that had made possible the stadium for the 1972 Munich Olympics, designed by Frei Otto and Günther Behnisch. The groundbreaking, lightweight design is based on

a 20-metre-wide (66 feet) shaft, which is kept in compression and secured to the ground by a net of pre-stressed cables. According to online technology magazine *New Atlas*, 'the tower shaft will have a height-to-width aspect ratio of around 80:1, considerably larger than that of the British Airways i360 in Brighton, UK, which is currently recognized as the world's most slender tower.' The structure will support a natural ecosystem: from base to apex, it will be covered by plants and inhabited by hundreds of animal species. The design team envisions 'the visual and social impact of New York's Central Park contained within the tower's footprint'.

The High Line

James Corner Field Operations, Diller Scofidio + Renfro, Piet Oudolf / New York, NY

From 1934 to 1980, this elevated railway – famously saved from demolition by a non-profit organization to become a public park and a major catalyst for the area's gentrification – used to carry freight trains 9.1 metres (30 feet) above Manhattan's largest industrial district. After the train traffic had been discontinued for good, the High Line, as it became known, remained an industrial ruin for almost twenty-five years, becoming gradually overgrown by self-seeded plants and out of bounds to everyone but the hardiest of urban explorers. The completion of the aerial park took five years and three phases, and attracted some 2 million visitors in its first year alone. The park that ribbons its way across twenty-two blocks, cuts through buildings and soars over streets has become one of New York's most popular attractions, inspiring a wave of similar infrastructure-revitalization schemes in other cities around the world.

The project was co-developed by New York-based architectural firm Diller Scofidio + Renfro and landscape architects James Corner Field Operations, together with Dutch garden designer Piet Oudolf. The key design decision was to refrain from architectural statements – to 'save the High Line from architecture', as Ricardo Scofidio puts it. Instead, the team focused on maintaining the best of what was already there: the melancholy of a post-industrial site; the surreal atmosphere of a secret garden in the midst of one of the word's busiest cities; and the striking yet unseen views of New York to be had along the entire length of the 2.3-kilometre (1½-mile) park. A great deal of effort has been spent on maximizing the experience, by maintaining such original features as the rails and facilitating the views. Custom-designed paving makes it easy for plants to break through, blurring the boundary between the garden and the path.

The High Line presented a genuine challenge for a landscape architect. In addition to being exposed to very hot summers and cold winters, it could accommodate only a thin layer of soil, thereby providing very little water and nutrients for the plants. The design team retained some of the High Line's self-seeded vegetation and sourced additional stress-resistant species from equally tough environments. A period of testing allowed the robust plants to be kept and those that did not survive to be replaced. The paving system was designed to retain between 80 and 90 per cent of the rainwater it receives.

The Lowline

Raad Studio, Mathews Nielsen, John Mini Distinctive Landscapes / New York, NY

Growing a subterranean park is a whole new field of horticulture. To determine which plants would survive underground, a group of experts led by Signe Nielsen, John Mini Distinctive Landscapes and Brooklyn Botanic Garden considered a whole list of factors, including temperature, humidity, light levels, water needs, colour and texture. The complex topography of the test site caters to plants that require low, average or high levels of light.

While SHoP Architects are upgrading the Essex Crossing on Manhattan's Lower East Side, James Ramsey and Dan Barasch have set their sights on the defunct trolley-car terminal located beneath neighbouring Delancey Street. They have an ambitious plan to transform it into the world's first subterranean park, the Lowline.

Ramsey, who studied cathedral design and worked as a satellite engineer for NASA before launching a career in architecture, used his knowledge of natural light and sophisticated optics to develop a key aspect of the project – namely, the Remote Skylight system, which will harvest the light of the sun for the Lowline's vegetation. Given that plants depend on photosynthesis for their survival, finding a way to deliver natural light underground was crucial. Even the most efficient electric lighting would fail to provide either the full spectrum of wavelengths present in sunlight or its intensity.

Opened in late 2015, the Lowline Lab was a critical step in bringing the project to life. The lab was set up in a warehouse, whose dim environment mimicked the actual site. Produced in cooperation with SunPortal, experts in fibre-optic daylighting, the Remote Skylight proved successful: the lab became home to a few dozen plants, including pineapple and strawberry – just a fraction of the future park, meant to spread across 5,570 square metres (60,000 square feet) and live off 100 sunlight collectors.

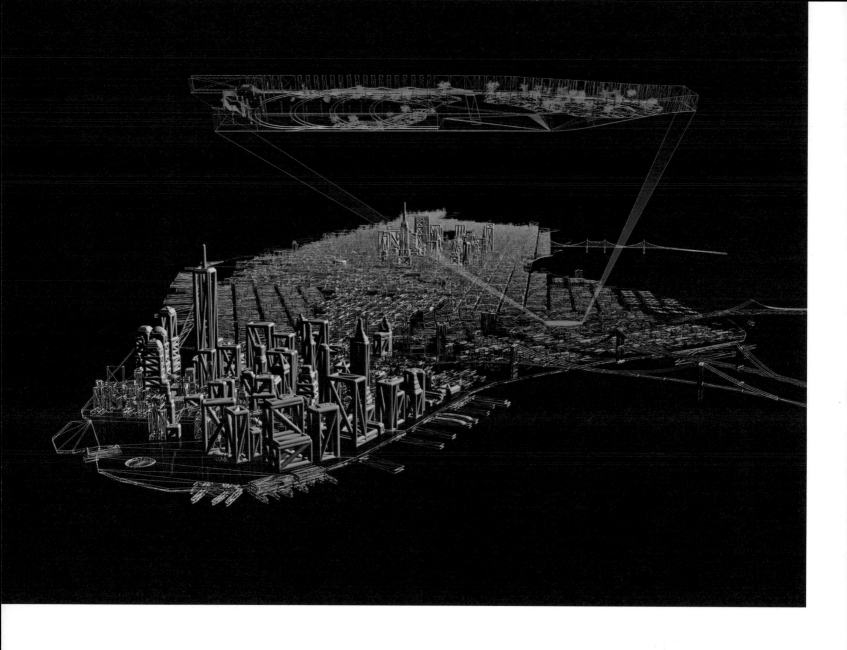

Subject to a lengthy test in the Lowline Lab (right and below), the Remote Skylight system uses tracking mirrors to capture sunlight, and parabolic reflectors that concentrate the light to nearly thirty times its normal intensity while filtering out infrared rays to prevent the device from overheating. Optical systems then steer this condensed light to specific underground locations. There, an aluminium canopy reflects and distributes the full-spectrum light that is vital to the plants' survival.

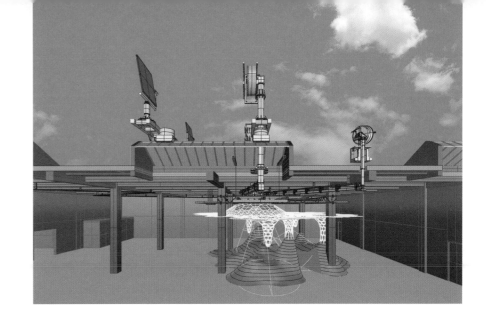

Asfalto Mon Amour

Coloco / Lecce, Italy

Over a period of two years, a team of architects and landscape experts from Paris-based studio Coloco staged a series of autumn and spring workshops in Lecce, Italy. Defined by Coloco as 'creative hybridization labs', these workshops involved landscape designers, farmers, gardeners, agronomists, actors, dancers and film-makers. Beginning with body-awareness exercises followed by brainstorming and debates, each day culminated in a few hours of intense physical work, such as construction, gardening and performance. Inspired by the slogan 'Asfalto Mon Amour', the participants were literally breaking up asphalt to transform a 2-hectare (5-acre) car park into a garden.

Located near Manifatture Knos – an abandoned metallurgical-engineering school repurposed into a cultural centre – the car park offered an excellent test site for Coloco's 'call to action' strategy. Strong believers in the power of physical involvement, as well as in shared authorship and shared responsibility, Coloco's founders Nicolas Bonnenfant and brothers Pablo and Miguel Georgieff have organized similar projects in various cities across France, from Montpellier and Marseilles to Paris and its suburbs. Neighbourhood residents, but also local officials, experts, creatives, activists and anyone else who feels like joining in, are invited to participate and improve a patch of the city. Much of Coloco's work relies on this alternative approach to urban transformation and the regeneration of public spaces, and consists in uniting groups of people around modestly sized projects and demonstrating how their collective efforts can produce real change. Small changes take time to add up to a bigger result – but the garden, too, takes time to grow.

Third Landscape Gardens

Coloco and Gilles Clément / Saint-Nazaire, France

Coined by French landscape designer, botanist and writer Gilles Clément, the term 'third landscape' refers to all kinds of leftover spaces – from wastelands to roadsides and railway embankments – but also to inaccessible and non-cultivable areas, as well as such protected zones as nature reserves. Not controlled by humans, these third landscapes provide 'a refuge for biodiversity'.

Deployed on the rooftop of a former submarine base – a vestige of the Second World War – in Saint-Nazaire, France, the Third Landscape Gardens, co-created by Clément, Coloco and a team of volunteers, are composed of the third-landscape plants of the Loire estuary and a selection of species that can grow on soil-less surfaces.

There are three parts to the gardens. The 107 trees of the Aspen Forest flutter above the disused detonation chambers. Semi-concealed inside those chambers, the Sedum Garden grows alongside a shallow canal and features a number of plants capable of thriving on concrete. Finally, the spontaneous Garden of Labels occupies one of the rooftop's recesses. Here, plants from wind-blown or bird-distributed seeds are identified and labelled as they sprout from a thin layer of soil.

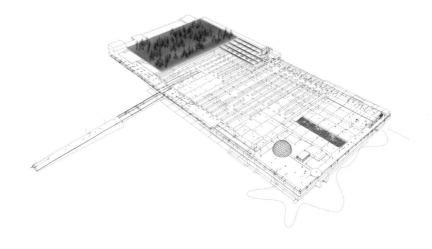

Sunken Garden

Plasma Studio / Beijing, China

A former landfill being rejuvenated by horticultural means, Beijing Garden Expo Park is the work of many architects and artists. Each team, having been allocated a share of the 513-hectare (1,268-acre) site, was tasked with creating a garden that would offer a new take on the area's cultural heritage while serving its ecological rehabilitation as well as the popularization of science. Seeking to design a garden in which a sense of intimacy and intensity would combine to produce a harmonious, contemplative experience, one of the participating teams, Plasma Studio, found a solution in the concept of the sunken garden.

Drawing inspiration from the Classical Gardens of Suzhou, a UNESCO World Heritage site, Plasma took such key elements of the gardens as the rock, the outcrop and the grotto 'to then travel in space and time to the image of hanging gardens and further on to the concept of a sunken courtyard'. The result is a man-made landscape to be experienced from below, from above, and from the inside. Measuring 1,000 square metres (10,780 square feet), the plot is structured by two intersecting corridors that guide visitors between a series of 'pocket landscapes', or micro-gardens. One of the corridors feels like a canyon flanked by oversized, irregularly shaped concrete planters, while the other takes you above the sunken parts of the garden. The labyrinth of pocket landscapes resembles a group of islands in the sea; some of them can be accessed via shaded ramps that change the 'user experience' from being surrounded by concrete and cor-ten steel to enjoying the shelter of a vegetal canopy.

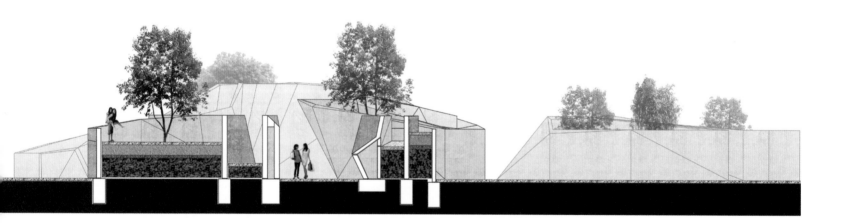

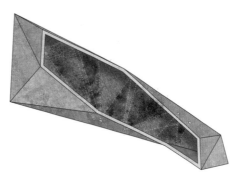

In the Sunken Garden, plants either grow on walled-in patches of raised ground accessible via ramps, or are hidden inside closed 'pockets', to be peeked at through pinholes drilled in the tall concrete walls.

Croton Water Filtration Plant

Grimshaw Architects, Ken Smith Workshop, Rana Creek / Bronx, NY

With buildable space at a premium, pollution levels high, and purification processes complex and expensive, New York City is looking for novel, hybrid ways of cleansing its water. Nature-based systems are being added to so-called grey infrastructures, and recreational uses layered over industrial ones. Writing in *Landscape Architecture Magazine*, Alex Ulam observed: 'In the past, water infrastructure projects had engineering firms calling most of the shots. The new approach involves multidisciplinary teams in which landscape architects and park planners play key roles.'

Designed by Grimshaw Architects and Ken Smith Workshop, the new Croton Water Filtration Plant, a state-of-the-art water-treatment facility in New York's Bronx, is seen as an exemplary project. The Croton System, the oldest of the three systems that supply New York with drinking water, meets some 10 per cent of the average daily demand. The new plant comprises six underground floors covered by a 3.6-hectare (9-acre) 'living roof', which serves as a driving range; it also happens to be the largest green roof in North America. It gives back to the city the municipal golf course that was destroyed in order to build the new water facility. To create this engineered landscape, Ken Smith collaborated with ecological design firm Rana Creek. As load restrictions for the extra-large roof limited the depth of the soil, the design team used structural polystyrene to sculpt the gently undulating topography that conceals the facility's vents and exhaust tubes. Bluestone and gabion security walls are integrated into the natural topography of the site; a system of ponds will collect rainwater. 'All surface water will flow naturally, led by gravity without the use of pumps, pipes or valves', note Grimshaw Architects, while Ken Smith emphasizes that, unlike conventional golf courses that rely heavily on chemical substances, their driving range will be maintained exclusively by organic means.

The Foundry Garden

Doazan + Hirschberger / Nantes, France

Once home to a thriving shipbuilding industry, the Île de Nantes fell into decline after the industry moved out of the area. Since the 2000s, however, this 350-hectare (865-acre) brownfield site in the heart of Nantes – one of France's oldest harbour cities – has been transformed into a new urban centre. Preserving its industrial heritage and giving it a new purpose are fundamental to the regeneration scheme. Thus, the garden designed by Doazan + Hirschberger occupies the 3,200-square-metre (34,440-square-foot) remains of a foundry. Before the company's transfer to another location, the facility produced marine propellers, including for the SS *France*, the world's longest passenger ship for more than forty years. Today, surrounded by a mix of office and housing, the foundry's naked metal structure forms the centrepiece of a public square.

The landscaping project consists of two kinds of garden. The grasses and bamboo shoots of the 'furnace garden' flock around the old machinery and partly spill over into the square. The idea was to highlight the vestiges of the past without creating the feeling of a museum. The remaining eleven bays of the 115-metre-long (377 feet) structure have been taken over by the 'voyage garden', a collection of imported plants that had originally entered Europe through Atlantic ports as the spoils of scientific expeditions. The intention, say the designers, was not to create a botanical garden but to gather in one place the 'traveller' plants – rhododendrons, hydrangeas, magnolias, camellias – that, although they came from far away, no longer feel exotic since they have become part of our environment.

Besides the former foundry's
metal skeleton, the garden
incorporates a number of other
features that refer to the site's
industrial past: old furnaces, rail
tracks, a bridge crane, and the
furnace pits that are now planted
with reed. Clear polycarbonate
roofing with a number of openings
has been added to the otherwise bare
structure. In addition to providing
humidity control, the roofing enabled
the use of plants suited to a much
warmer climate, giving the garden
a 'singular and exotic' feel.

MFO-Park

Burckhardt+Partner, Raderschall Landschaftsarchitekten / Zurich, Switzerland

A different take on the vertical-park concept, this project was co-designed by two Swiss firms, Burckhardt+Partner and Raderschall landscape architects, as part of a radical plan to redevelop a former industrial zone in northern Zurich and turn it into a mixed-use district known as New Oerlikon. The masterplan for the area included a series of small public parks intended to serve as both places of relaxation and landmarks to aid orientation.

Built on a site occupied until 1999 by the century-old engineering firm Maschinenfabrik Oerlikon (MFO) – at one time Zurich's biggest employer – the MFO-Park takes the form of a three-dimensional plaza that doubles as an event hall. The new park is, in fact, a 17-metre-tall (56 feet) 'urban arbour' overgrown with sprawling plants and offering the experience of a walk-on sculpture. According to Burckhardt+Partner, abundant foliage lends 'a precise architectural body' to the open steel frame that encloses an atrium-like garden space with a sun deck on top. The interstices between the framework's double walls are open to exploration, incorporating stairways, walkways and balconies cantilevered over the 'atrium'. Subtly yet clearly, the hangar-like form and proportions of this 'park house' refer to the area's industrial past, when it used to be a kind of Forbidden City accessible only to factory employees.

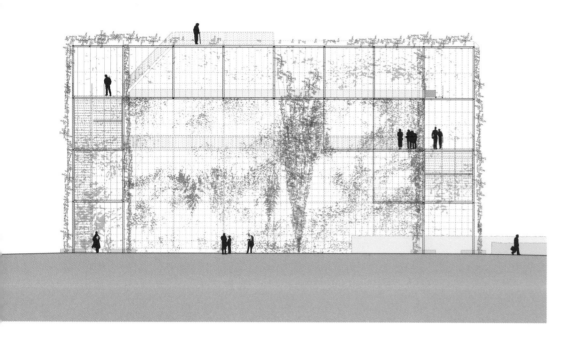

Shaped by a steel framework 100 metres (328 feet) long and six storeys high, the MFO-Park sets the record for the world's largest pergola. In this truly vertical landscape, the vegetation touches the ground only lightly. More than a hundred species of woody vines and creepers climb up the industrial steel cables, arranged so that each vine has a cable of its own. The use of deciduous plants highlights seasonal change. In summer, the structure completely vanishes behind green foliage; in autumn, the foliage is thinner but adds reds and yellows to the colour palette; and in winter, the rigour of the steel frame is made visible to all.

Coexistence

Coexistence

When Peter Zumthor commented on his walled-garden design for the Serpentine Gallery Pavilion 2011, the Swiss architect's fascination with plants was eloquently expressed: 'Plants embody everything that I like to have around me: presence, personality, character. They are supple and therefore strong, yet softly spoken and gentle; they are fragrant and delicate; they have movement, colour, structure, scale and proportion. Plants are large in form, tiny in detail and always a single whole.' Writing about the use of plants in *A Pattern Language* (1977), architect and design theorist Christopher Alexander was no less enthusiastic: 'People need contact with trees and plants and water. In some way, which is hard to express, people are able to be more whole in the presence of nature, are able to go deeper into themselves, and are somehow able to draw sustaining energy from the life of plants and trees and water.' The designs showcased in this chapter maximize such contact to the point where people and plants are literally sharing the same space.

Many of these schemes are vivid design statements. Aided by a team of volunteer 'constructor gardeners', Marco Casagrande has transformed an abandoned sugar factory in Taitung, Taiwan, into a knowledge-sharing platform for people to cohabit with plants (page 148). Parts of the roof are open to the sky, thus ensuring that the plants receive sufficient water. In designing a mixed-use tower in Beirut, Lina Ghotmeh condensed the distinguishing traits of the Lebanese capital's complex fabric into a single building (page 115). A tree growing in the middle of an atrium-like kitchen offers a witty contribution to the nostalgic 'old Saigon' feel of a contemporary Vietnamese house by a21studio (page 136).

Resonances between the client brief and the architect's own agenda give rise to striking design solutions. Thus, Andrew Maynard and Mark Austin's idea of a 'half-ruined' house invaded by vegetation (page 145) was the product of a family's desire for a home with a strong inside–outside element; the architects' dismay at the 'banality' of many contemporary housing projects; and a shared desire for environmentally sustainable living. Similarly, the design for the Bathyard Home by Spanish firm Husos (page 133) resulted from the client's demand for a big bathroom and a space for accommodating her numerous plants combined with the creative team's search for more efficient uses of the small patios and light wells that are present in so many apartments in Madrid.

The creation of transitional spaces and the exploration of their psychological and functional potential is another prominent theme in many of these projects. On the border between the city and the jungle, Divooe Zein has built a sequence of 'transparency layers' in a showroom and event space that, while feeling like a safe, peaceful shelter, nevertheless remains highly permeable and open to nature (page 116). The 'space for the plants' that envelops the living room of the House in Moriyama (page 140) is not just architect Makoto Tanijiri's response to the 'house-plus-garden' brief for a drab location; it is also an invitation to the residents, who have furnished the space with artworks and books and regularly cross it to access other rooms, to truly coexist with the plants. In the shared learning centre for the Paris-Saclay educational and research 'cluster', co-designed by Sou Fujimoto, Nicolas Laisné and Manal Rachdi (page 124), the light-filled, landscape-like atrium will help facilitate the cross-disciplinary encounters that are proving pivotal to the future of research and education.

In his *Book of Tea* (1906), Japanese scholar Kakuzo Okakura praised tea masters for creating places of serenity in the midst of the city and making their guests feel as if they were 'in the forest far away from the dust and din of civilization'. Today, such architects as Fujimoto or Junya Ishigami are focused on the boundary between the oasis of one's home and the bustling street, between architecture and landscape, replacing a partition with a gradient to render such a border porous and nebulous. A project for the Venice Biennale and a house for a young couple (page 152) embody Ishigami's quest for an environment in which, to quote his book *Plants & Architecture* (2008), 'nature comes close enough to be indistinguishable from architecture'. This is going to be 'a new, more inclusive version of architecture that transcends rigid concepts of the city. Subtle and supple spaces that imperceptibly bridge architecture to the things around us.'

House Before House

Sou Fujimoto / Utsunomiya, Japan

In 2008 Tokyo Gas, Japan's largest natural-gas supplier, invited architects Terunobu Fujimori, Toyo Ito, Sou Fujimoto and Taira Nishizawa to design four concept houses. The brief was to create 'a primitive home of the future', with stronger connections to nature and opportunities for the residents to awaken each of their senses, as opposed to the increasingly uniform and sensory-neutral apartments of today's cities.

Fujimoto proposed 'a new concept of a domestic space' that stemmed from his reflections on the notion of a home not being equal to a house. Arguing that a home is not limited to the indoor area, he divided a regular house into several parts

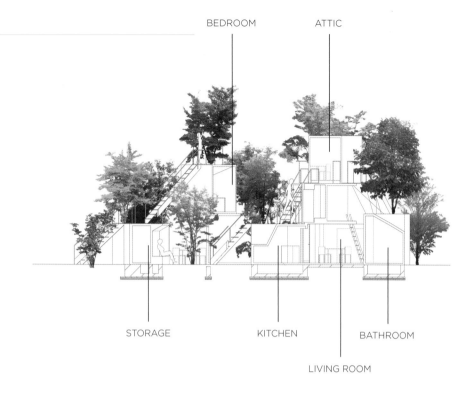

BEDROOM ATTIC

STORAGE KITCHEN BATHROOM

LIVING ROOM

and reassembled them into a complex arrangement of smaller 'boxes', each big enough to contain a single room. The inside and the outside thus became one continuous space. By planting trees on top of the boxes and carefully planning the voids and connections between each volume, Fujimoto created a home by means of various 'spaces for people', rather than rooms. Residents may touch the top of a tree that grows just beneath their feet; cross a stepped bridge to get from one room to another, as if they were climbing up a hill; or daydream on the roof of their bedroom under a 'floating tree'. In this way, a house becomes similar to a village, or to a landscape that grows organically over time.

Commenting on his design, Fujimoto described it as an attempt to reach back to our distant past, when houses and forests were one and the same space, and recreate a kind of 'small Earth that would be the most primitive and yet the most futuristic architecture'.

Stone Gardens

Lina Ghotmeh – Architecture / Beirut, Lebanon

Designed by Lina Ghotmeh (formerly of DGT Architects), this tall, monolithic volume with textured façades and variously sized apertures brimming with greenery is an architectural comment on the scarred history of her hometown, Beirut. 'Violence has left traces on the skin of [the city's] buildings', says Ghotmeh. 'It has reshaped and hollowed them. Overgrown concrete skeletons change our concept of an "opening" on the facade.' Together with the concrete masses of new-build apartments and the few remaining traditional, tile-roofed houses, these ruins – which, ironically, are just about the only green spots in the city – form the urban fabric of the Lebanese capital.

It is to this mix that Lebanese photographer Fouad Elkoury decided to add a new building with a sense of timelessness. The family-owned site was once home to the Middle East's first concrete company, founded by Fouad's great-grandfather, and, later, to the office of his father, the renowned Lebanese architect Pierre el-Khoury. The surroundings, too, are remarkable, with the port district rapidly being transformed into a vibrant creative hub while still maintaining the rough charm of a former industrial area. Ghotmeh's thirteen-storey tower comprises a series of apartments aimed at young professionals and design aficionados, as well as the Arab Center for Architecture, a foundation established to raise public awareness of architecture and urban design. As if carved out of a chunk of earth, it resonates with the raw open-endedness of the city and makes greenery an important part of its identity.

With marine views on every floor, the project's uniquely laid-out apartments are provided with their own 'urban gardens'. These gardens come in a variety of shapes and sizes, from the double-height 'Jungle' to an individual, shade-giving 'Tree' and the 'Plant', a glimpse of green that inhabits the smaller openings.

Siu Siu

Divooe Zein / Taipei, Taiwan

At the core of architectural design, believes Taiwan-based architect Divooe Zein, is an exploration of the connection between humans, plants and the environment. Built on one of Taipei's wooded mountain slopes, Siu Siu, or the Laboratory of Primitive Senses, is exemplary of Zein's approach to architecture. The project was largely inspired by the Shinano Primitive Sense Art Festival in Japan, which brings together traditional culture and contemporary art. Home to a showroom and a variety of workshops, cultural events and spiritual practices, Siu Siu was designed as a transitional space between the city and the forest.

'We didn't do many shop drawings', explains Zein. 'Instead, we made design decisions on site.' Acknowledging that contemporary working styles require little interior space, since most tasks can be done on one's portable digital device, the design team built a solid enclosure only for the areas that had to be sheltered 'in earnest', such as the showroom, the reception area and the toilet. These were placed inside a wooden-and-glass cabin that integrates the remains of an old farmhouse. Its flat roof forms a mezzanine used for yoga and meditation, and is directly connected to the higher part of the slope. All of this is overarched by a translucent,

tunnel-like shelter, open on both ends and incorporating not only the built elements but also the space around them, together with trees and other plants.

The shape of this 8-metre-high (26 feet) tunnel follows the site's complex topography, while its structure replicates the greenhouse design commonly used in Taiwan. Its light metal framework is covered with agricultural netting, which serves as a sunshade, absorbs ultraviolet light and allows for natural ventilation. Moreover, the tunnel offers reliable weather protection, and creates a pleasant microclimate for humans and plants alike. Subtropical light passes through the double filter of the foliage and the agricultural netting, emulating 'the poetic atmosphere of ancient Chinese paintings' as it gently illuminates the workshop area and the meditation deck.

The project's external shelter is composed of a framework of thin metal rods covered with two layers of black agricultural netting – providing a 60 per cent shading rate on the inside and 80 per cent on the outside – and a waterproof membrane sandwiched between them. Easy to build and low-impact, the structure is flexible enough to accommodate a number of existing trees.

Optical Glass House

Hiroshi Nakamura & NAP / **Hiroshima, Japan**

The water basin in the main garden serves as a skylight for the entry space below. When leaves flicker in the wind, or rain falls on the surface of the pool, rippling patterns appear on the entrance lobby's floor.

Hiroshi Nakamura's design transforms a bustling street, complete with cars and trams, into a silent background for an urban oasis. To neutralize the busy thoroughfare just beyond the client's front door, the architect used layers of delicate filters to create a sense of tranquility inside the house. Composed of 6,000 bricks – painstakingly cast from extremely clear borosilicate glass and invisibly reinforced to form a stable wall – the front façade both screens the interior from the street and reveals it. Sunlight is refracted through the bricks, which, depending on the time of day, can appear transparent or translucent. Perceived as a vision rather than an exhibit behind the glass wall, a roofless internal garden opens directly into the main living space, from which it can be separated by means of a featherweight metal-mesh curtain.

Additional gardens are located at the rear of the house. The kitchen/dining room forms an open-plan layout with the living room, thus facilitating air flow between the front and back gardens and providing ample natural ventilation. On the upper floor the main bathroom faces an olive garden, while the secluded tatami room on the ground floor connects to a garden inhabited by stewartias, with their reddish bark and white, camellia-like flowers.

The open-plan layout of the living
and dining rooms on the first floor
connects the maple and ivy gardens
at the front and back of the house –
with the very practical advantage of
providing plenty of natural ventilation.

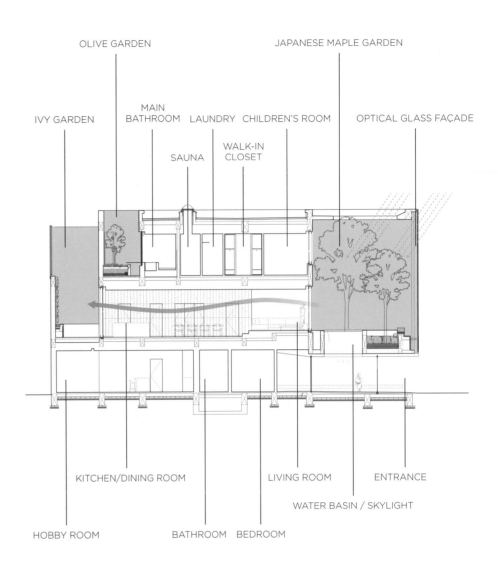

OLIVE GARDEN

JAPANESE MAPLE GARDEN

IVY GARDEN

MAIN
BATHROOM   LAUNDRY   CHILDREN'S ROOM   OPTICAL GLASS FAÇADE

SAUNA   WALK-IN
CLOSET

KITCHEN/DINING ROOM   LIVING ROOM   ENTRANCE

WATER BASIN / SKYLIGHT

HOBBY ROOM   BATHROOM   BEDROOM

Shared Learning Centre

Sou Fujimoto, Manal Rachdi OXO Architects, Laisné Roussel / Paris-Saclay, France

By 2020, Paris-Saclay – a large cluster of educational and research facilities located to the south of the French capital – is expected to accommodate ten major schools, ten research institutes and three universities. The cluster's new learning centre, commissioned by École Polytechnique with the intention of sharing it between six leading graduate schools and research institutions, reflects the continuing shift towards the kind of cross-disciplinary collaborations that are recognized as the future of innovation. Architects, too, are part of the story, as it is their task to provide environments that will foster what digital-innovation expert Greg Satell has called the 'ecosystems of talent, technology and information'.

Perhaps not surprisingly, the winning proposal for the shared learning centre is a collaborative project by three architectural firms. The key element of the scheme is the front part of the building, designed to encourage spontaneous encounters, interactions and exchanges. This light-filled, atrium-like space is formed by interconnected walkways, platforms and staircases that double as tiered seating; classrooms can be opened up towards the communal areas. Tall but slender trees and a fully glazed façade measuring 17.8 metres (58 feet) in height connect the building to a vast lawn at the front, which serves as a magnet for drawing people towards the centre. Sou Fujimoto describes the overall mood of the building as 'an invitation to enter, wander and meander; to be more involved with these spaces', while Manal Rachdi, the third member of the design team with Fujimoto and Nicolas Laisné, is convinced that their project will generate new, future-oriented modes of teaching and learning.

At the shared learning centre, say its architects, 'encounters will no longer take place in corridors, but in animated spaces, in a setting bathed in gentle light, with views and perspectives that change and surprise'. Designed with particular attention to lighting and acoustics, the project creates a sense of peaceful, comfortable shelter suitable for large gatherings and small group meetings alike.

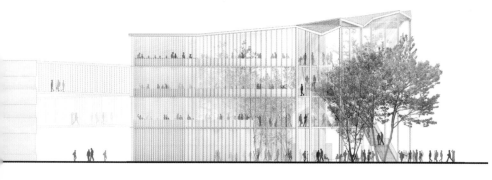

House N

Sou Fujimoto / Oita, Japan

'Architecture', says Sou Fujimoto in his book *Primitive Future* (2008), 'exists in how exteriority and interiority are connected.' Featuring an internal garden, House N is just one possible manifestation of the Japanese architect's vision of a 'house of the future', with its 'nebulous' environment that has no clear border between the interior and the exterior. Instead, exterior space is created through layering multiple interior spaces and gradually opening them up.

Designed for a couple and their dog, the house consists of three white concrete boxes arranged one inside the other, so that the interior of one volume becomes the exterior of the next. The largest box – or 'shell', as Fujimoto calls it – circumscribes the 176-square-metre (1,894-square-foot) plot and accommodates the semi-indoor garden. The second shell forms a more 'interiorized' space, while the third, innermost enclosure defines the core of the house, an 18-square-metre (194-square-foot) living and dining room. Only the windows of the middle volume are glazed. The garden is placed closest to the street, while the kitchen and bathroom occupy the same interstice between the external and middle volumes but at the rear of the house. Tucked between the middle and inner volumes are the entrance hall, bedroom and tatami room.

The residents' privacy is protected through the considerate placement of windows. Other than that, the structure is very open to the outside, and the layout is almost exclusively defined by the limits of the three shells, with no additional partitions.

A total of forty-four rectangular windows and skylights pierce the triple shell of House N. Their size and placement provide the optimal combination of natural lighting, views and privacy. The nested boxes range in height from 7.3 metres (24 feet) – the maximum allowed by the local building code – for the external box to a more human-scale 2.7 metres (9 feet) for the innermost box.

KITCHEN   LIVING ROOM

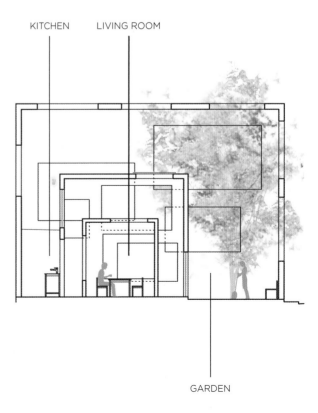

GARDEN

Bathyard Home

Husos / Madrid, Spain

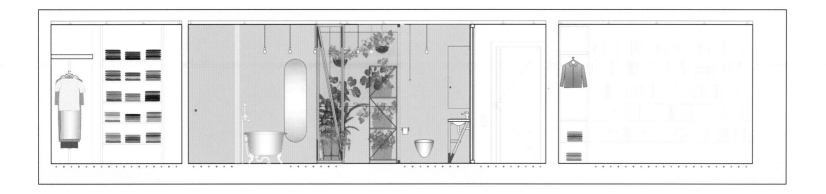

Designed 'for a woman, her family and her plants', the Bathyard Home provides a comfortable environment for each of these in what was originally a dark and energy-inefficient apartment. The project, by Spanish architectural firm Husos, transforms two of the owner's dreams – to have a spacious bathroom, and to keep some of the plants she used to have in her former suburban house – into an energy-savvy design.

In the architects' own words, Bathyard Home was an opportunity to give a new 'climatic and social dimension' to the kinds of secondary spaces – narrow patios and light wells among them – that are common to many of the residential buildings in and around Madrid and other Mediterranean cities. With a few simple modifications, the design team made the most of the single south-facing window in this 130-square-metre (1,400-square-foot) apartment, which is now entirely oriented towards the south. Originally, this window overlooked the patio, and was wasted on a corridor and storage area.

The 'bathyard' (opposite) has movable partitions with different levels of transparency, while the door to the walk-in closet incorporates a folding bench – design elements that allow for a varying degree of privacy and enable the roomy, plant-populated bathroom to be turned into a socializing space. The living room (right) features an oculus, which makes use of an existing hole in the load-bearing wall. Today, it connects the living room to the bathyard, both visually and climatically.

The new scheme integrates the window into a unique kind of space, with all other rooms focused around it. The architects call this space a 'bathyard', explaining that it 'generates a new "exterior" inside the apartment, and lends passive thermal and light comfort to the entire home'.

The owner's ferns, rubber plants and marantas populate a small greenhouse, whose strategic location in the centre of the bathyard, right between two wet areas – a bathtub space and a more private shower and toilet – ensures sufficient humidity for the plants. The greenhouse, the only place in the apartment that doesn't use underfloor heating so as not to dry the air out, is kept warm through its southern exposure and contact with other rooms. The bathyard's central position, say the architects, facilitates cross-ventilation and enjoyment of the new, south-facing 'landscape'. They also say that, with its smart layout and improved overall insulation, the Bathyard Home boasts a temperature of 18–20°C (64–68°F) on most winter days, without the need to turn on the heating.

Saigon House

a21studio / Ho Chi Minh City, Vietnam

Although a recent addition to the block, Saigon House looks older than many of its neighbours. The reason for this is rooted in the client brief. Ms Du, a native of Saigon (as Ho Chi Minh City was known prior to 1975), needed a house for her family, but also a place where her siblings could get together and relive their childhood memories – and where *their* children could develop happy memories of their own. She did not, however, want a Western-style house of the kind that is currently popular in Vietnam, but which to her feels faceless and stirs no emotions. The architects at a21studio shared this mindset, as well as a love of Saigon's stacked

roofs; its flowering balconies that open on to courtyards; its rich diversity of building materials; and the 'colourful clutter' of its traditional neighbourhoods. All of this is present in their design. Located on a long and narrow plot, it has four levels of individual rooms shaped as small houses and cantilevered above the kitchen/dining room, in which the whole family gathers. A tree at its centre strengthens the outdoor feel and evokes a typical Saigonese alley. More plants grow on the balconies and burst through the steel latticework of the street façade. Children love the house, especially the net over the kitchen/dining room, which creates a thrilling playground.

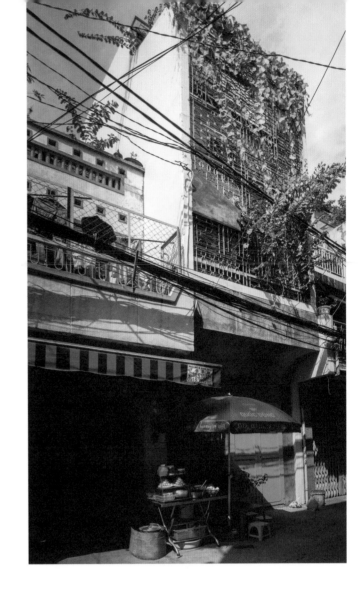

The project gives new life to materials salvaged from demolished Saigon properties. Rooms shaped as individual houses have sloped tile roofs – a feature typical of old Saigon – while the ground-floor kitchen/ dining room feels like a courtyard.

House in Moriyama

Suppose Design Office / Nagoya, Japan

A family with two children commissioned Suppose Design Office to design a house with a thriving garden on a site that looked hardly suitable for the task. The narrow plot was too small to accommodate a garden next to a house, while its location – a tight slot between other buildings in Nagoya's industrial area – was quite problematic in terms of natural light and outdoor views.

In order to conjure up a pleasant domestic environment in such unwelcoming surroundings, architect Makoto Tanijiri moved the entire garden inside the house and created a 'garden room', which he interlocked with other spaces. The garden begins as soon as one enters the house, wraps around the living and dining room, and opens into the upper-level bedroom through a series of light wells, which provide the residence with most of its natural light. In his design for the house, Tanijiri has gone beyond simply inviting the outdoors indoors; rather, in order to strengthen the connection between the 'space for the plants' and the 'space for the people', he has treated the garden like any other room – to the point where the family has furnished it with artworks, books and other objects.

With a compact footprint of just 42 square metres (452 square feet), this landscaped and light-filled design creates a 'breathing' and constantly changing kind of home.

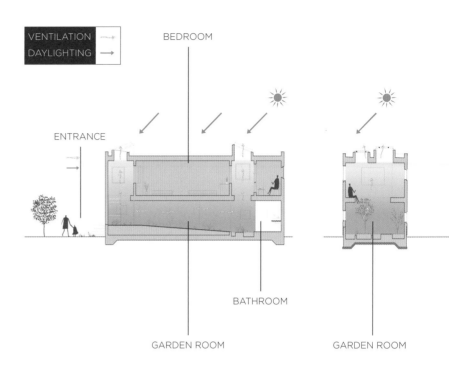

VENTILATION

DAYLIGHTING

BEDROOM

ENTRANCE

BATHROOM

GARDEN ROOM

GARDEN ROOM

With its light wells, the
'garden room' opens
the house to natural light
and ventilation. Moreover,
it envelops the living
spaces with a kind of
'atmospheric layer', thus
ensuring comfortable
room temperatures.

Cut Paw Paw

Austin Maynard Architects / Melbourne, Australia

This house got its indoor garden as a consequence of the client wanting 'a strong connection between inside and outside' – a brief that the architects, Melbourne-based Andrew Maynard and Mark Austin, took very seriously. Commissioned to renovate and extend a double-fronted weatherboard home, they chose to leave the structure unfinished. Explaining their decision, the design team evoke the often disappointing contrast between a house under construction and after completion. 'When wandering the street and stumbling on an anonymous house in construction, we all get excited by the possibilities. We imagine what the finished building could be like. The site holds so much promise when there is nothing more than a timber or steel frame. Often, it is when a building is at its most beautiful.'

Unfortunately, it is all too common for the finished building not to realize the potential displayed by its naked skeleton. In fact, for the architects, such a building 'will not again be interesting until it eventually begins to crumble and decay'. With the Cut Paw Paw house, however, the situation is very different. Between the properly roofed and clad dining area and the music studio at its other end, the entire central part of the building is an unclad frame, into which the garden enters without obstruction. 'It is both inside and outside,' say the architects. 'It is both a new building and an old ruin.'

Responding to the client's request for a sustainable home, the design team opted to 'do more with less' and, wherever possible, keep the old rather than replace it. The house incorporates such green features as abundant insulation and rain-water management, while the architects have used the daily and seasonal path of the sun to determine the arrangement of open and shaded areas. The positions of windows and doors facilitate natural ventilation and optimize solar gain, thereby minimizing the need for mechanical heating and cooling.

Ruin Academy Taitung

Casagrande Laboratory / Taitung, Taiwan

Intended as an open platform for cross-disciplinary research, the first Ruin Academy was launched by the architect and environmental artist Marco Casagrande in Taipei, Taiwan. In 2010 Casagrande and a team of volunteers, who called themselves 'constructor gardeners', brought to life an empty building awaiting redevelopment. They removed interior partitions and window frames, and drilled a series of circular openings in the roof and the floor slabs in order to let in both air and rain. Between 2010 and 2012, groups of 'academic squatters' shared the building with greenery planted on every floor.

The Taitung Ruin Academy was set up in 2014 as part of the Taiwan Design Expo. Established by the constructor gardeners in an abandoned sugar factory, the Taitung academy was focused on exploring the local knowledge of Taiwan's indigenous peoples and ways of applying it to the ecological restoration of cities. The core of the academy was centred around the factory's evaporator tanks, with a plan gradually to expand it over the entire facility. Multipurpose spaces for workshops and studios were coupled with community gardens and patches of wild plantation. Fragments of the roof were removed so that the rain could fall on the planted areas; the roof's remaining parts and drainage channels were used to harvest rainwater for irrigation. Communal spaces included lounges with open fireplaces and a tatami room for group meetings, exercise, meditation and rest. Floors covered with either wooden planks or earth encouraged visitors to walk barefoot.

Following the end of
the design expo, the
abandoned factory that
housed the academy was
sealed for a few years
to allow the vegetation
to take over, with plans to
reopen it at a later date.

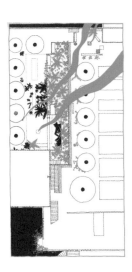

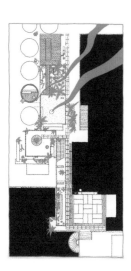

Extreme Nature

Junya Ishigami / Venice, Italy

What if our buildings and cities were designed so that the boundary between nature and architecture became almost impossible to detect? When Junya Ishigami imagines such a scenario, he is interested neither in nature-inspired designs nor in engineered landscapes, but in the opportunity to treat 'architectural' and 'natural' spaces as equals. 'I would like to regard plant life not just as a landscape element,' says Ishigami in his book *Small Images* (2012), 'but as an element that is equivalent to buildings in the way they form a space.' At the same time, his aim is to bring a building to the state of 'ultimate transparency', right on the border 'between existence and non-existence'.

Ishigami's interests came together in his project for the 2008 Venice Architecture Biennale, at which the Japanese architect represented his country. Together with structural engineer Jun Sato and botanist Hideaki Oba, he built four 'greenhouses' in the garden of the Japanese Pavilion. Wanting the structures and the plants to have 'an equal presence', he designed each greenhouse as a slender frame with walls and ceilings in crystal-like glass and columns that emulated the proportions of the plants. Indoor and outdoor vegetation merged into a single landscape; furniture was scattered across the garden to further blur the boundary between landscape and interior design. The result, as described by curator Taro Igarashi, was a 'unique spatial condition' that allowed visitors to experience 'the simultaneous coexistence of plants, furniture, buildings, landforms, all things inside and out'.

House with Plants

Junya Ishigami / Tokyo, Japan

In this house for a young couple, Junya Ishigami has put into practice some of the ideas he developed for the Venice Architecture Biennale in 2008 (see pages 152–3). Back then, Ishigami proposed a series of conceptual projects in which he revised the relationship between architecture and landscape by combining both to create what he called 'ambiguous spaces'; these spaces brought the inside and the outside 'infinitely close' to each other, but 'never allowed the two to assimilate'. Among the projects he developed were a holiday home in the city and a bachelor pad, both of which engaged in a lively dialogue with their surroundings. In the latter project, the ground floor – a single, extremely transparent,

semi-outdoor room – hosted an 'inner garden' that spilled out into a thick mini-forest occupying the entire plot. A small bedroom was tucked upstairs, while the bathroom was placed in a separate structure.

Located in Tokyo, House with Plants follows a very similar pattern. Its thin-walled, double-height, cuboid form with large glazed openings appears to enclose part of an existing garden. Stepping stones in the exposed earth lead to a closet in the corner, while a kitchen block, complete with dining table, cupboard and fridge, sits on an irregularly shaped patch of flooring. The living room is housed in a smaller box-within-a-box structure, whose roof doubles as a bedroom.

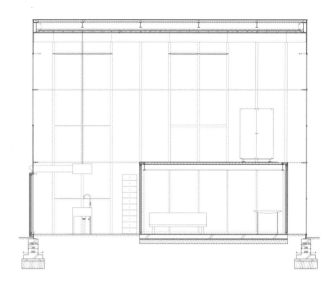

Atelier Tenjinyama

Takashi Fujino – Ikimono Architects / Takasaki, Japan

In Takasaki, Japan, where thunderstorms are frequent in summer and dry winds blow on clear winter days, Takashi Fujino has designed a live/work space for himself that might be described as a piece of 'primitive', experience-based architecture. A constant connection to nature being central to the project, the structure itself remains fairly simple. Four concrete walls – each 18 centimetres (7 inches) thick but none strictly rectangular – extra-large glazed openings and a ceiling of shatterproof glass provide just the right amount of physical comfort, but are extremely generous in the way they engage all of the senses.

'I create a box to live in; install a window to be connected to the town and a transparent roof to look up at the blue sky; plant trees to get shade; make a soil floor for the roots to grow; and raise the ceiling for the trees to thrive,' explains Fujino, the name of whose practice, Ikimono, translates into English as 'being alive'. The open-plan, 62-square-metre (667-square-foot) space – with just a partition screen to separate the living and work areas – boasts an 8-metre-high (26 feet) ceiling and is populated by all sorts of plants, of which an evergreen lemon-scented gum takes centre stage. Fujino claims that, living here, he has come to realize the psychological benefits of plants. To him, the sight of continuous growth and change offers as much encouragement as seeing a growing child who learns new things every day.

Takashi Fujino treats plants as architectural materials, placing them according to the qualities he wants to lend to a space. In the case of Atelier Tenjinyama, the foliage of trees provides shade in summer; a lemon-scented gum and lemon myrtle add fragrance to the air; and jasmine grows next to the kitchen and scents the tea. The plants grow naturally and get their nourishment straight from the ground. In exchange, says Fujino, they give something back in terms of sight, sound, touch, smell and taste.

Performance

Performance

This chapter looks at the ways in which nature can endow a building, or even an entire city block, with an element of performance. It highlights three sometimes overlapping threads: projects with bioclimatic features; buildings that improve biodiversity; and 'productive' architecture. As before, the focus is on how these innovations shape the architecture of the city.

Urban projects that rely on nature's 'utility value' – that is, its capacity to improve air and water quality, regulate microclimates, facilitate stormwater management and reduce noise – range from city-scale strategies to specific parts of a building. A few such projects have already been discussed: think of House for Trees by Vo Trong Nghia (page 18), a prototype bioclimatic design intended for future replication, or the Croton Water Filtration Plant by Grimshaw and Ken Smith (page 96), an example of hybrid infrastructure in which a man-made landscape conceals the roof of a major underground facility, returns the site to its original use as a golf course, and enables stormwater management and phytoremediation (the removal of contaminants through the use of plants). Among the projects considered in this chapter is Harmonia 57 by Triptyque Architecture (page 166). Responding to its location in a frequently flooded part of São Paulo, Brazil, this artists' residence incorporates a rainwater harvesting system, highlighting its operation by means of exposed tubes and the apparently untamed vegetation that bursts through the 'pores' in its concrete façades.

Over the next two decades, the city of Copenhagen plans to realize 300 projects aimed at dealing with the consequences of climate change, especially increased rainfall. Urban development consultants SLA have helped the city council devise a new strategy to ensure that all of these climate-adaption projects draw on nature-based solutions. In addition, notes SLA's Kristoffer Holm Pedersen, as the city's density increases, its residents are becoming ever more concerned about pollution, hence 'a growing need for wise urban planning so that the city can self-purify the air, water and soil, while managing rainwater, regulating temperatures, etc.'.

At the other end of the spectrum, scale-wise, is the Active Modular Phytoremediation wall, co-developed by Skidmore, Owings & Merrill (SOM) and Rensselaer Polytechnic Institute (page 170) as a plant-based and more efficient alternative to air-conditioning systems for offices.

Architecture can also be used to increase and maintain biodiversity. Urban ecologist Philippe Clergeau believes that, in order to be environmentally friendly and foster biodiversity, the city should densify rather than sprawl. 'Green corridors' could then be used to connect such larger natural habitats as parks and forests with scattered smaller nodes, creating a unified ecological network. Édouard François's residential tower designed to serve as a biodiversity junction in a former industrial district (page 179); his budget-conscious scheme that has turned a social-housing block into a garden by 'simply' allowing nature to take care of itself (page 175); and the mixed-use building by Husos that has evolved into a true environmental lab (page 182) are just a few examples of how biodiversity concerns can play a crucial role in shaping an architectural project.

'Cities should be productive even in times of recession,' says Anouk Legendre, co-founder of XTU Architects, whose creatives dedicate a large part of their practice to realizing exactly this goal. With years of research under their collective belt, Paris-based SOA Architectes and Laboratoire d'Urbanisme Agricole (LUA) have a vision for reforming the city-making process, in which farming is elevated from a 'victim of the urban sprawl' to 'one of the city's structural components'. Some of SOA's proposals (page 194), as well as XTU's pioneering productive façade system (page 204), are featured in this chapter. Further projects in which architecture meets urban farming have set out to explore other facets of the subject. The headquarters of the recruiting firm Pasona (page 190), where employees share their workspace with vegetable beds, was intended as a green building capable of changing not only people's daily routines but also their life choices; sleek Plantagon skyscrapers (page 200) strive for maximum efficiency as they integrate new-generation, industrial-scale greenhouses with office property; while the projects by Lina Ghotmeh (page 186) and Ilimelgo (page 198) combine organic food production with the functions of a cultural venue and community centre.

Harmonia 57

Triptyque Architecture / São Paulo, Brazil

The design concept for this artists' residence was shaped as much by climate-related issues as by the dynamic transformation of Vila Madalena, São Paulo's bohemian district. Guillaume Sibaud, a partner at Triptyque Architecture, refers to the area's curious architectural juxtapositions and aesthetic clashes – qualities that found their way into the project, in which smooth-surfaced, minimalist interiors contrast with rough exterior design.

Challenged to build in an area that is prone to flooding during the rainy season, but which lacked efficient means of retaining water, Triptyque applied their creative nous to draining the site and putting harvested rainwater to good use. For Harmonia 57, rainwater is both a source of non-potable water (for use in the building's toilets, for example) and a means of climate control. A system of sprinklers irrigates the plants that sprout through the 'pores' in the façades, thereby cooling the building. In contrast to the perfectly manicured vertical gardens one often sees, Harmonia 57 proudly reveals its plastic tubing and other low-tech paraphernalia – the vascular system of a building designed as a living organism that 'breathes, sweats, ages, recovers and changes over time'.

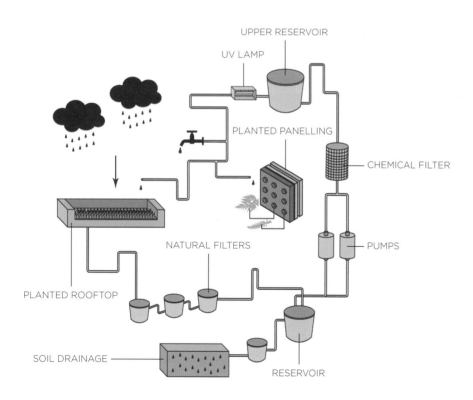

UPPER RESERVOIR

UV LAMP

PLANTED PANELLING

CHEMICAL FILTER

NATURAL FILTERS

PUMPS

PLANTED ROOFTOP

SOIL DRAINAGE

RESERVOIR

The network of tubes, filters and sprinklers that facilitates the harvesting of rainwater is an important design element. Some of the tubes double as guard rails, while the exposure of the entire system highlights the processes that support life on the building's façades.

Venha
conhecer
a nossa
Irmãzinha

A nossa
Irmã mais
nova
veio morar
com a gente!

AMPS Wall

CASE – Skidmore, Owings & Merrill and Rensselaer Polytechnic Institute

ACTIVE BIO- AND PHYTO-FILTRATION   PLENUM-DUCT MODULE

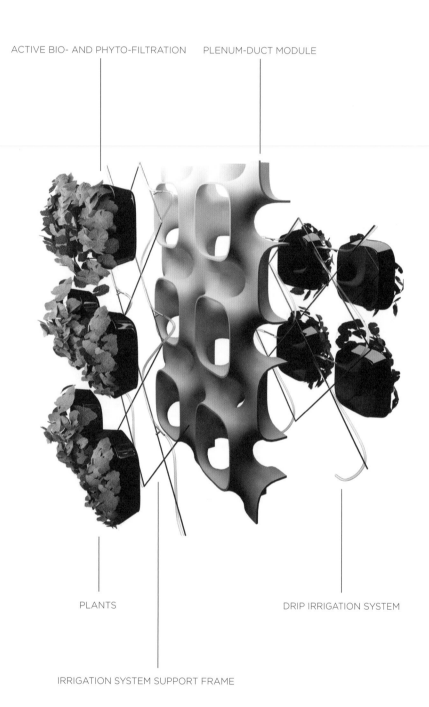

PLANTS

DRIP IRRIGATION SYSTEM

IRRIGATION SYSTEM SUPPORT FRAME

The employees at the new Public Safety Answering Center in the Bronx, New York (opposite, top), will be the first to benefit from the real-life application of AMPS, a wall system that uses live plants to radically improve indoor air quality. Developed by CASE – a research unit co-founded by Skidmore, Owings & Merrill architects and Rensselaer Polytechnic Institute, focused on next-generation sustainable building technologies – AMPS addresses the inability of air-conditioning systems to filter out or neutralize the toxins given off by office equipment, furniture, paint and carpeting. Moreover, add the architects, 'the outdoor air that these systems draw in is often more polluted than the indoor air.'

AMPS (short for Active Modular Phytoremediation System) is designed to exploit the air-cleansing capacity of plants. Many of us are aware that a plant's foliage can neutralize pollutants and increase oxygen levels. That the area around its roots has a cleansing capacity 200 times greater is less well known. With AMPS, hydroponically grown plants are placed in a vacuum-moulded, double-sided, self-supporting structure. Its modules are shaped so as to minimize the use of material while maximizing the airflow and exposure of the roots. Tests confirm that, in a typical office, AMPS would lower the levels of volatile organic compounds by 80 per cent, thereby significantly reducing the need for energy-consuming mechanical ventilation.

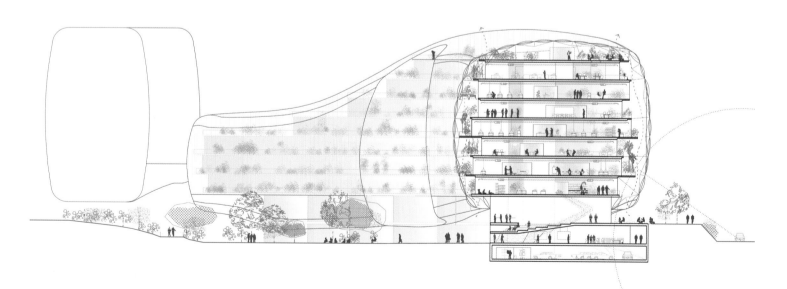

Drivhus

SelgasCano, Urban Design / Stockholm, Sweden

The winter view of Stockholm's proposed Planning and Administrative Offices (below) is particularly compelling. The competition-winning design by Spanish architects SelgasCano and their Swedish colleagues Urban Design packs a 'working environment for 1,800 people, as well as a space for civil servants, politicians and the public to meet and discuss the future development of the city', inside a multistorey greenhouse under a transparent hood. Known as Drivhus (the Swedish for 'greenhouse'), the project will be located beside Stockholm Globe City, a large entertainment district from which nature is visibly absent. A mixed-use development with a park is planned for the area, and Drivhus will invite greenery not only into its courtyard but also 'under its skin'.

The idea to provide the project with a 'bioclimatic façade' was born of an analysis of the climate and its predicted changes. For Stockholm, the global increase in erratic weather patterns will mean shorter winters and warmer, more humid summers. Designed to last a hundred years, Drivhus is ready to face the challenges ahead. Its double-skin façade consists of an exterior shell made from ETFE air cushions and an interior wall in glass, with plants inhabiting the space in between. Probably best known for its use in Nicholas Grimshaw's Eden Project in Cornwall, England, ETFE plastic is strong, lightweight and super-transparent. It absorbs infrared light, reducing the building's energy consumption; softens interior acoustics; and is easy to replace at the end of its fifty-year lifespan. A combination of the ETFE shell and a flexible natural-ventilation system will create a tempered microclimate for a whole range of plants: potted lemon trees; plants grown by the employees; tomatoes, fruit and herbs cultivated for the facility's restaurants; and the contents of the park's mini-nursery. Visible and accessible from the workspaces, all this vegetation will offer a stimulating work environment and a healthy break from office routine.

Eden Bio

Édouard François / Paris, France

The fact that the client behind Les Vignoles, the social-housing project designed by Édouard François, could not afford the regular maintenance of green spaces did not discourage the architect from including them. The issue was resolved by helping nature take care of itself. Nicknamed 'Eden Bio', the project was designed 'not as a landscape, but rather as an abandoned territory that is colonized by plants', explains François, whose most significant contribution to the growing of Eden Bio's gardens was the replacement of the existing polluted soil with bio-certified organic earth, on which 'any wind-blown seed would explode'. Wisteria, the only deliberately planted species, has quickly invaded the wooden staircases and scaffolding that covers the façade of the long central building; otherwise, the resulting landscape has developed completely spontaneously. Three years after the project's delivery, the area was populated by young, 2-metre-high (6½ feet) trees and other plants, while some tenants had put to good use the empty flower pots left for them on windowsills and balconies. Built to honour the area's agricultural past, two greenhouses host the bicycle shed and – in the hope, says François, that their surroundings will mitigate the effect of occasional bad news – the letter boxes.

Once a suburban
settlement, this area
of Paris is today part
of the inner city. Eden
Bio's design scheme
honours the area's
past, maintaining
the low height of the
houses, as well as
the long and narrow
alleyways between them.
Vegetation occupies
the corridors and
recesses of this 'porous',
village-like setting.

Biodiversity Towers

Édouard François / Nantes and Paris, France

In 2011, when Paris City Council revised its decades-long ban on high-rises and allowed tall buildings to be constructed in some of its new development areas, Édouard François was among the first architects to design a residential tower in a former industrial district undergoing massive regeneration. In fact, his 50-metre-high (164 feet) scheme dealt with two issues at once, proposing an intelligently planted façade that would both mitigate Parisians' aversion to living in high-rises and lower the building's environmental impact. Moreover, François's M6B2 tower (opposite) was intended as a proactive design that would restore and increase biodiversity in the city. The density of the planting on M6B2 – comparable to a wooded hill within the city – increases towards the top of the building, which will use its height to distribute seeds across a large portion of Paris (the image at the bottom of page 181 gives a sense of how far they might reach). Add its proximity to several railways, and you have an important junction in the area's much needed 'green corridor'.

Crucial to the scheme was the selection of only the hardiest and most adaptable of species. This was done in collaboration with expert botanists and students from the École du Breuil, Paris's school of horticulture. Seeds of wild plants collected in the forests around Paris were cultivated in tough conditions, with no fertilization and minimal watering, before being transferred to M6B2's bespoke planters as the project was completed in 2016.

A knowledge of chasmophytes
(plants that grow in the crevices
of rocks) proved crucial when it
came to minimizing the planters'
size and weight. Tested at the École
de Breuil, stainless-steel tubes
measuring 3.5 metres (11½ feet) long
and 0.35 metres (1 foot) wide were
eventually used to accommodate the
plants – many of them chasmophytes.

A similar design – airy balconies
protected by metal mesh and
incorporating plants growing in steel
tubes – was proposed for François's
earlier scheme, the Planted Tower
of Nantes (page 179 and below, top).
In this unbuilt project, a residential
tower doubles as a showcase for
rare plants – namely, IUCN Red
List species grown at the Botanical
Garden of Nantes.

Host & Nectar Garden Building

Husos / Cali, Colombia

The practice of having a home and a business under one roof is an old tradition in Cali, Colombia. What's new about this particular project is that it throws a biodiversity hotspot into the mix. The idea was conceived jointly by the project's client and architects, together with the biologist Francisco Amaro and other collaborators, including Cali Zoo.

Commissioned from Husos architects by Taller Croquis, at the time a small but growing fashion house, the building was designed to accommodate various uses and be adaptable to change. With circulation corridors running between the building's main wall and the metal mesh that forms its outer skin, all spaces could be entered and rented out individually. Moreover, the mesh could be used to support a lush growth of climbing plants, which have since immersed the residents in local flora.

Apart from providing passive climate control and an almost rural charm, the vegetation used for the outer skin and inner garden was chosen to serve as host plants and a source of nectar for butterflies, insects and birds. Colombia is home to 10 per cent of the earth's biodiversity, while up to 45 per cent of the country's own flora and fauna is concentrated in the province of which Cali is the capital. Sadly, local species of plants have less presence in the new development areas, and people know little about their land's unique natural heritage. The team behind the Host & Nectar Garden Building is therefore on a mission to spread information (and seed packets) to encourage Caleños to broaden the city's network of self-managed gardens.

According to Husos's own description of the project, 'The building uses the presence of butterflies as a biometer to gauge the quality of the environment.' The architects go on to explain that butterflies – highly dependent on specific host plants, but also very sensitive to variations in temperature, humidity and light – are one of the best indicators of man-made changes to the environment. Fittingly, Colombia is home to one of the greatest diversities of butterflies in the world.

Réalimenter Masséna

Lina Ghotmeh – Architecture / Paris, France

Countless research laboratories around the world are working hard to address the challenge of feeding the earth's population, which is expected to number 9 billion by 2050. Yet many people are unaware of these efforts and the solutions proposed by experts. Which is why, in her winning proposal for the Reinventing Paris competition, architect Lina Ghotmeh suggested converting Paris's disused Masséna railway station into a showcase for 'the food of tomorrow'.

A gathering place for local residents and a destination for foodies, Réalimenter Masséna will bring together urban farmers, researchers, chefs, artists and the media to help foster a food culture and raise awareness of the ways in which our food is grown and produced. The former railway station will be complemented by a tower, the first in Paris to be built from wood – and, no doubt, to host such a wide range of food-related activities.

The two interconnected buildings will house 750 square metres (8,073 square feet) of urban farms, as well as educational workshops, an interactive canteen, a food market, a concert venue, a street-art gallery and a few residential units. Having every step of the food-production process – 'from plough to fork' – represented in one place will help to promote a zero-waste policy. A spiral ramp will connect the tower's thirteen floors, reinforcing the project's collaborative spirit.

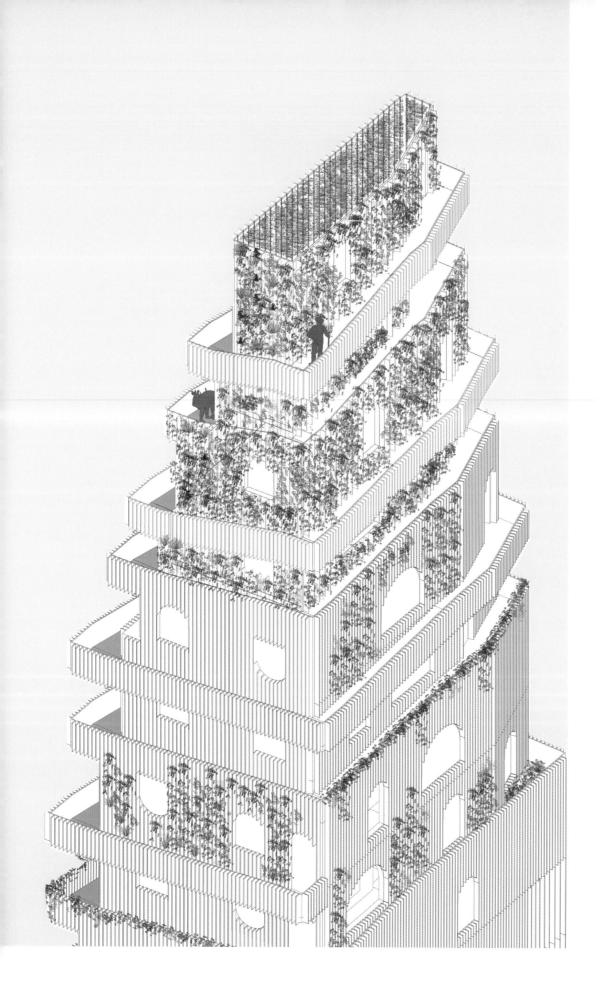

Dedicated to urban farming, the top three floors of the wooden tower will be entrusted to AgroParisTech (a Paris-based university specializing in life sciences and agronomy) and Sous les Fraises (urban farmers of organic vegetables). Half of the project's total area will be occupied by research, entertainment and retail spaces, while 25 per cent will be given over to housing, including flats for the resident chef, artist and researcher. The spiral ramp will incorporate planters, so that the residents, too, can grow food.

Pasona HQ

Kono Designs / Tokyo, Japan

One shouldn't be surprised to learn that Pasona Group has combined its new headquarters in downtown Tokyo with a farm – literally. For a company that, since its inception, has been focused on generating rewarding job opportunities for such individuals as housewives, young people and seniors, it was only natural that it should offer its own employees a healthy experience, enabling them to spend their working week surrounded by plant life and enjoying fresh greens in the office cafeteria. The design concept, by New York-based Kono Designs, put forward the idea that crops and office workers should share the same space. Thus, a rice paddy and a broccoli field can be found in the main lobby; pumpkins grow in the reception area; a canopy of tomatoes hangs above the conference tables; salad leaves sit on hydroponic trays in the seminar room; while beans sprout in the drawers that are smartly tucked under the meeting-room benches.

Instead of constructing a new building, Pasona chose to renovate an existing, fifty-year-old structure, which now boasts a double-skin façade with seasonal flowers and orange trees planted on the 90-centimetre-deep (3 feet) balconies. While the office-farm initiative is about well-being and education, rather than economic efficiency, the bioclimatic effect of the green façade nevertheless reduces heating and air-conditioning costs. Growth lamps require additional energy, but at the same time the office lighting scheme reduces energy consumption by 30 per cent compared to more conventional options. In addition to creating a better work environment, Pasona uses its office farm as part of a project to promote contemporary forms of agriculture. With farming in steady decline in Japan, the company wants to show the next generation that it can be an innovative and profitable business.

Japan's largest and most direct farm-to-table office scheme was given form by Kono Designs. The green spaces at Pasona HQ total 3,995 square metres (43,000 square feet) – some 20 per cent of the entire building – and are home to 200 species of plant, including fruits, vegetables and rice. The architects point out that, owing to a lack of arable land, Japan has become the world's biggest importer of food, with more than 50 million tons brought in annually, which, on average, are transported over 14,484 kilometres (9,000 miles). Pasona's practice of growing and consuming food inside the same building represents a possible solution to reducing 'food mileage'.

Vertical Farms

SOA Architectes

Mostly unknown to the public but occupying large amounts of peri-urban land (the area between the suburbs and the countryside), soilless agriculture is often housed in hangar-like facilities that – together with business and industrial parks – add to the creation of generic and monotonous landscapes. Why not, asked Augustin Rosenstiehl, a partner at the Paris-based architectural firm SOA, consider moving this agricultural production into the city? An important part of SOA's work is dedicated to exploring 'vertical farms' from architectural and urban-planning perspectives. How can farms be integrated into the dense urban fabric? What kind of architecture would fit the purpose both functionally and aesthetically? And how compatible are the technical requirements of intensive farming with the need to protect a city's cultural heritage?

In an attempt to answer these questions, SOA interviewed a range of experts – juxtaposing architectural, social, economic, environmental, cultural and food-related concerns – before devising a series of proposals. One of these was the Urbanana building (opposite and page 197), a combined plantation, research lab and exhibition space for the development and promotion of the cultivation of bananas

In a study commissioned by the French town of Romainville, SOA looked into the possibility of combining the town's urban renewal project with the development of local fruit and vegetable production. SOA's proposal (above) grafts on to the top of existing housing blocks a structure composed of interconnected year-round greenhouses. Circulation and service spaces are anchored to one of the lateral façades.

in mainland France. Such facilities would use growth lamps rather than natural lighting, and could therefore be inserted into narrow 'leftover' spaces between other buildings. Its transparent front façade would expose a 'hanging garden' of banana trees, while the lighting necessary for their growth could save the city a few street lights. Cactus (page 194 and opposite, top right) packs its plantations into modules clustered around a tall mast. With a minimized footprint and shadow, the structure – based on the principle of tensegrity – would capture natural light from every angle. Another proposal, the totem-like, 300-metre-high (984 feet) Tridi Farm (opposite, bottom right), is large enough to house agricultural production on an industrial scale. Having no floor plates, this mechanically operated farm relies on a three-dimensional, mesh-like structure, which would allow natural light deep into its heart. Entirely concealed by plants, the towering construction would appear as a striking aerial garden, a production facility celebrated as a landmark.

Market Garden Tower

Ilimelgo and Secousses / Romainville, France

Life in Romainville, a suburban town that is now part of Greater Paris and is being integrated into new transport networks, is about to get more dynamic. Since the area has always had strong agricultural roots, urban farming sits at the top of the list of long-term plans for the local economy. Among the pilot projects is the Market Garden Tower. Designed by Ilimelgo and Secousses architects on a site that belongs to the public-housing agency, it is intended to enable the local production of fresh food, create jobs and liven up the neighbourhood. More than 1,000 square metres (10,764 square feet) of plant beds filled with organic substrate rather than soil will be stacked inside a transparent facility complete with an educational greenhouse and a direct sales shop. The design team opted for archetypal shapes, and matched the project's height to the surrounding buildings. The project relies on prefabricated elements, and features a double-volume design with an all-glass exterior to maximize natural lighting. Green features include composting, rainwater management and a façade with vent panes and roller blinds for natural ventilation and protection from solar heat gain.

Plantagon

Plantagon International with Sweco / Linköping, Sweden

Plantagon, an organization focused on making industrial-scale vertical urban farming not only possible but also efficient and aesthetically pleasing, has its first project under construction in Linköping, Sweden. The multi-functionality of Plantagon's hybrid tower is partly derived from the need to combine optimized industrial processes with climate control.

At the core of the project is the patented 'transportation spiral', which forms a production loop. Nourished by a hydroponic system, crops in both pots and trays move slowly down the spiral, reaching the basement level by the time they are ready for harvesting. The spiral structure minimizes the need for artificial lighting. Moreover, being within a façade system measuring between 3 and 6 metres (9¾ and 19½ feet) wide, it allows the building to be occupied by other functions – offices, in the case of the Linköping project – while providing sufficient levels of shade and daylight.

Together with Swedish architecture and engineering consultants Sweco, Plantagon has developed a range of designs geared to different locations and light conditions. Variations include globe-shaped facilities intended to make the most of the omnidirectional light of near-equatorial zones; 'Plantascraper' façades and tubular add-ons for existing towers; specifically lightweight structures with ETFE-pillow façades; stand-alone models dedicated entirely to the growing of food; and buildings designed to integrate a greenhouse with other functions right from the start.

The Swedish city of
Linköping will be home
to the world's first
Plantagon tower (right
and opposite). Here, the
company is using an
'integrated greenhouse'
model. Wrapped around
offices and a research
and development centre,
a cultivation area of
4,300 square metres
(46,285 square feet)
will sit within the façade
of a building with
a footprint almost
three times as small.

Biofaçade

XTU Architects

An interest in designing cost-efficient, productive buildings has led XTU Architects to the idea of turning urban façades into bioreactors for the growing of microalgae – arguably, one of the world's most useful raw materials. Populating oceans, lakes and watercourses, these micro-organisms produce, by means of photosynthesis, more than 75 per cent of our oxygen and remain one of the planet's most significant carbon sinks. Incredibly rich in proteins, lipids, antioxidants and other biologically formed molecules, microalgae have over the last few decades become increasingly popular in all sorts of fields, from healthcare and cosmetics to food and fodder production. They offer a valuable resource for green chemistry, and are actively being investigated as a prime material for the production of biofuel.

Developed by SymBIO2, a consortium of laboratories, start-ups and manufacturing companies formed by XTU, the biofaçade is an industrial-scale, profit-making microalgae farm integrated into a high-performance façade system. Patented in 2009, the flat, ultra-thin façades use wastewater to grow valuable biomass at 30 per cent of the usual cost; they also form a 'thermoregulation envelope', which can reduce by half the cost of heating and cooling a building. The first biofaçades will start operating in Paris as part of In Vivo (opposite), a new urban block designed by XTU and MU architects. There will be three towers: the Tree House, featuring large planted balconies; the Plant House, with loggias for small-scale urban farming; and the AlgoHouse, a residence for students and young researchers with biofaçades producing microalgae for medical research.

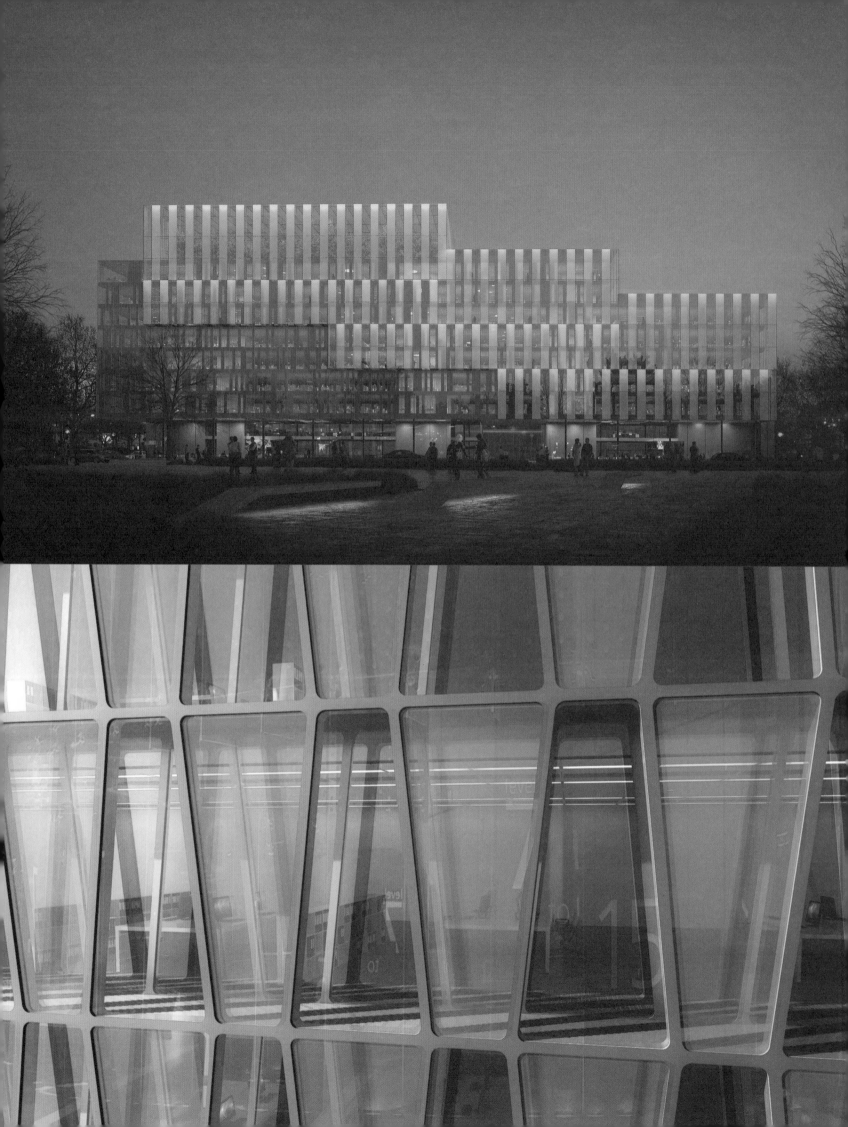

The biofaçade technology cultivates microalgae inside double-glazed façade cells filled with water. To ensure that they receive the optimum amount of daylight, as needed for photosynthesis, the algae are kept in constant motion by a system of hydraulics. Invisibly integrated into the façade's structure, the hydraulics circulate both water and air. The microalgae will be harvested on a nightly basis, as part of a digitally controlled maintenance cycle. Pictured right is AlgoNOMAD, a working prototype of the biofaçade installed in front of Paris City Hall.

Fusion 2.0

Fusion 2.0

While Le Corbusier imagined a house as a 'machine for living in', co-founder of XTU Architects Nicolas Desmazières would prefer it to be an 'organism for living in', a definition that chimes perfectly with each of the focal points of this final chapter, which tries to imagine what the next steps might be in bringing together nature and the city.

A pioneer of vertical green urbanism, Malaysian architect and ecologist Ken Yeang sees the architect's task as part of a much bigger challenge of bio-integration – that is, the need to integrate 'everything we do and make in our built environment (which ... consists of our buildings, facilities, infrastructure, products, refrigerators, toys, etc.) with the natural environment'. This can be achieved through 'ecomimesis', a design approach that emulates nature's processes, structures and functions to render human-made ecosystems compatible with natural ones, thereby enabling them 'to sustain life in the biosphere'.

The concept of cities as ecosystems is explored in many future-oriented designs in which architecture works in unison with nature. French landscape architects Coloco and New York-based artist, engineer and inventor Natalie Jeremijenko speak of 'mutualism' – a mutually beneficial relationship between different organisms – as one of the underlying principles in the organization of natural systems. 'We are part of a complex urban ecosystem,' says Jeremijenko, emphasizing that cities should be designed as 'multidimensional mutualistic interdependent systems' that ensure the well-being of humans and non-humans alike. Vincent Callebaut – some of whose science fiction-like designs are being realized in Taiwan, China, Egypt and Belgium – has a fantasy of turning New York into an Amazonian forest: 'Each tower is a tree; each tree produces energy and has its waste transformed into a resource for some other function. Different functions and ecosystems interact with one another to create an intelligent city that, like nature, knows neither pollution nor waste.' Over the next five years, Callebaut is going to work on 'transforming the city into a mature ecosystem'. Using information and communications technologies to drive architecture, his design process takes many of its cues from biology, since it involves biomimicry and bionics, in addition to incorporating actual vegetation. The case studies commissioned from Callebaut's office by Paris City Council (page 242) hint at what he has in store.

Architectural experimentation has 'zoomed in' to develop such growth-friendly building materials as green concrete (page 215), reconfiguring the bigger picture in an attempt to counterbalance the excess of 'inorganic content' with which we humans are filling the biosphere. Landscaped spiral ramps bring plants to the top of Ken Yeang's bioclimatic skyscrapers in an uninterrupted movement that creates 'vertical streets' while multiplying 'ecological linkages'. The team at Architensions proposes to apply the methods of vertical green urbanism to an entire city block (page 241), while Rael San Fratello venture even further, suggesting that sensor-equipped 'aerial gardens' be suspended from semi-autonomous airships to provide a kind of 'environmental ambulance' (page 236).

Seamless cooperation between natural and digital systems is another powerful concept that is likely to shape the city of the future. Examples include breathe.austria's enhanced forest (page 228) and Philippe Rahm and Catherine Mosbach's 'eco park', with its solar-powered, nature-inspired climatic devices (page 232). Claudia Pasquero and Marco Poletto of ecoLogicStudio (page 220) voice the idea of 'a curated dialogue' between biological and artificial systems, investigating the potential of such a dialogue in projects that range from art installations to collaborations with advanced research units seeking new uses for cutting-edge satellite monitoring technologies. 'Think about trees as the photosynthetic modules that branch at the ends, or as double branching systems if you add the underground part,' says Poletto. 'If you look at a forest, you might think about the ways the tree roots and the mushroom mycelia form a communications network, a sort of biological Internet. Suddenly, a tree is no longer a tree; today, we are able to understand it on different levels, because we have the Internet, which is not only a way of communicating, but also a way of understanding the world. I think it's time to make this step.'

Are we ready for take off?

Rising Canes

Penda

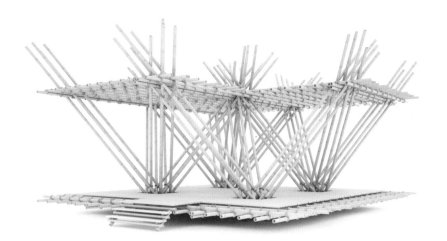

Chris Precht, co-founder of Beijing-based studio Penda, has a passion for scalable structural systems. His earlier designs included a diamond-shaped structural grid that could be used for both a pavilion in a park and a skyscraper in a metropolitan downtown.

In 2014, for a competition that promoted a sustainable approach to designing hotels in natural settings, Precht proposed a modular system derived from the construction of a tepee, which has since evolved into the Rising Canes project. This new system uses bamboo, which the design team regards as a remarkable if underrated building material with a wealth of local knowledge behind it. Bamboo matures within four to six years, grows up to 40 metres (131 feet) high, and is two to three times stronger than a steel beam of a similar weight. Moreover, since its root system remains alive, bamboo will regrow by itself after being harvested. Penda's design is based on X-shaped joints fastened with ropes. The joints are doubled to add stability, and interconnected by horizontal beams. A single module is 3.8 metres (12½ feet) high and 4.4 metres (14½ feet) wide. The resulting structure can expand in any direction, and the elevated ground floor means that it adapts to various landscapes.

Having shown a working prototype at Beijing Design Week 2015, Penda imagines that entire neighbourhoods could be built in this way, with bamboo groves planted nearby to ensure a constant supply of materials.

Green Concrete

XTU Architects

Paris-based XTU Architects have developed building materials that are capable of serving as natural supports for the growth and development of plants. From brick planters (opposite) – their first attempt at 'sprouting façades' – they moved on to the next generation of green wall, which would allow plants to grow directly out of the facade, without the need for a growing medium or integrated water-delivery system. 'We experimented with porous, granulated concrete,' says Anouk Legendre, a founding partner of XTU, 'for which the researchers at Paris-Sud University had picked out some two hundred plants that could grow on their own and without destroying the wall.'

A selection of drought-resistant, maintenance-free species, chemically compatible with concrete and capable of sequestering carbon dioxide and up to 40 per cent of atmospheric nitrogen – two of the main urban pollutants – promise to turn the structures built from this 'green concrete' into air purifiers on an architectural scale.

Urban Algae Follies

ecoLogicStudio

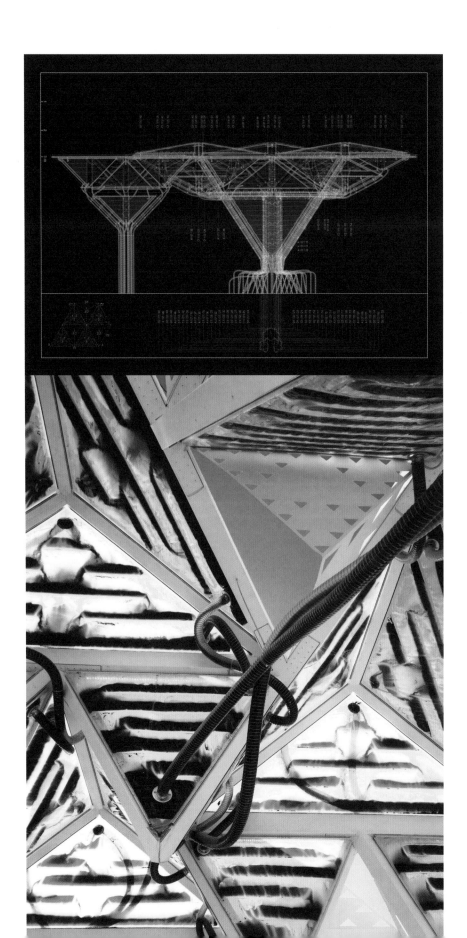

Marco Poletto and Claudia Pasquero of London-based ecoLogicStudio draw on advanced digital technologies to develop concepts and prototypes that blur the boundary between the natural and the artificial. They also explore the possibility of merging the built environment with biological organisms to form a 'co-evolutionary assemblage'.

Poletto and Pasquero's Urban Algae Follies integrate microalgae into built structures to create a new kind of architecture, 'a biodigital productive public space,' says Poletto. One such structure was designed for Milan's Future Food District at Expo 2015 (left), to demonstrate how algae farming can be effectively linked to a city's food and energy infrastructure.

Urban Algae Follies breed microalgae in bioreactors made from ETFE plastic; these, in turn, serve as building elements for new architecture – a canopy in the case of Expo 2015. Many of the project's constantly varying properties are the result of a complex set of relationships between climate, living organisms and digital control systems, with a real-time digital protocol linking algae growth to the weather and the movement of visitors. Sunshine, for example, triggers an increase in the flow of nutrients, water and CO_2 (the ingredients necessary for algae cultivation), causing more growth and increasing the canopy's potential to provide shade; the presence of people, meanwhile, causes electrovalves to alter the speed of the algal flow, affecting the canopy's transparency and colour.

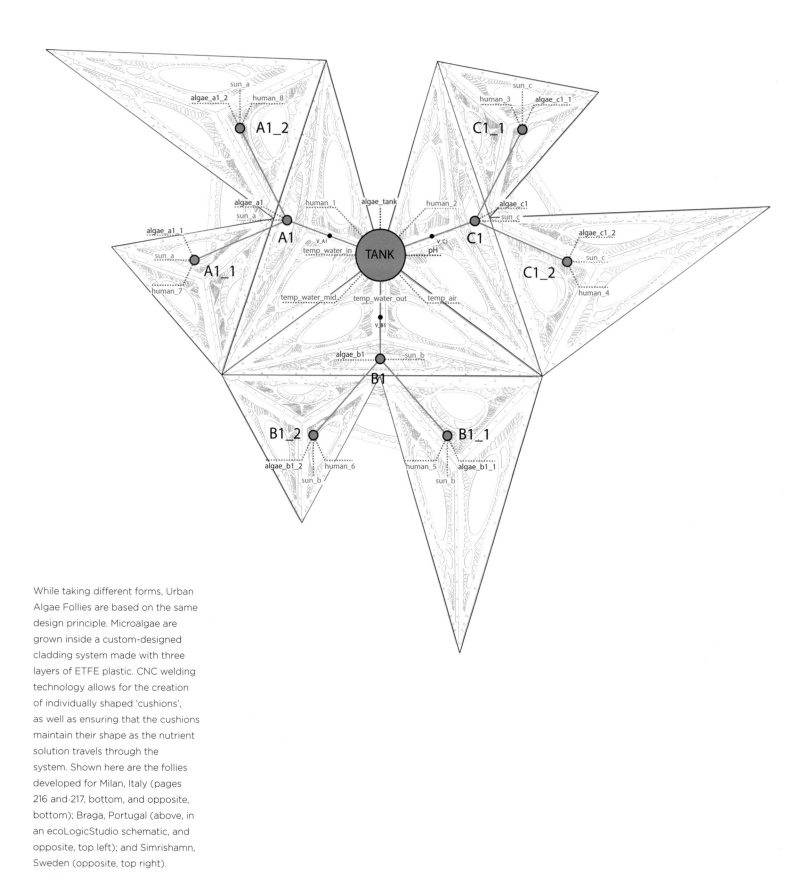

While taking different forms, Urban Algae Follies are based on the same design principle. Microalgae are grown inside a custom-designed cladding system made with three layers of ETFE plastic. CNC welding technology allows for the creation of individually shaped 'cushions', as well as ensuring that the cushions maintain their shape as the nutrient solution travels through the system. Shown here are the follies developed for Milan, Italy (pages 216 and 217, bottom, and opposite, bottom); Braga, Portugal (above, in an ecoLogicStudio schematic, and opposite, top left); and Simrishamn, Sweden (opposite, top right).

H.O.R.T.U.S.

ecoLogicStudio

'I don't mind covering a building with trees, but I'd be more intrigued if trees became a real part of a building – in a way that is not just trying to mimic trees on mountains, but rather creating a whole new sort of organism.' So says ecoLogicStudio's Marco Poletto, who believes that society is already ripe for 'a different kind of appreciating nature'. Developed by the studio for various exhibition venues, including London's AA School of Architecture, the EDF Foundation in Paris (below) and the Centre for Art and Media in Karlsruhe (opposite), H.O.R.T.U.S. (Hydro Organisms Responsive to Urban Stimuli) take photobioreactor design to a new, conceptual level. These sophisticated, tree-like installations are shaped by a mix of practical and educational requirements. They are fit for cultivating microalgae, but also, perhaps more importantly, use interactivity and aesthetics to open up the entire process to the public, to whom a typical microalgae farm might feel somewhat remote, 'ugly and a little scary'. When visitors breathe CO_2 into the transparent microalgae pods; scan the QR code to find out whether this particular species is used for food, energy or medical production; witness the different colours the algae take depending on their growth phase; or simply admire the way in which light shines through algae-filled water, they engage with a seemingly obscure processes on a personal, mostly non-verbal level, gaining a more profound understanding of the infrastructure that surrounds us all.

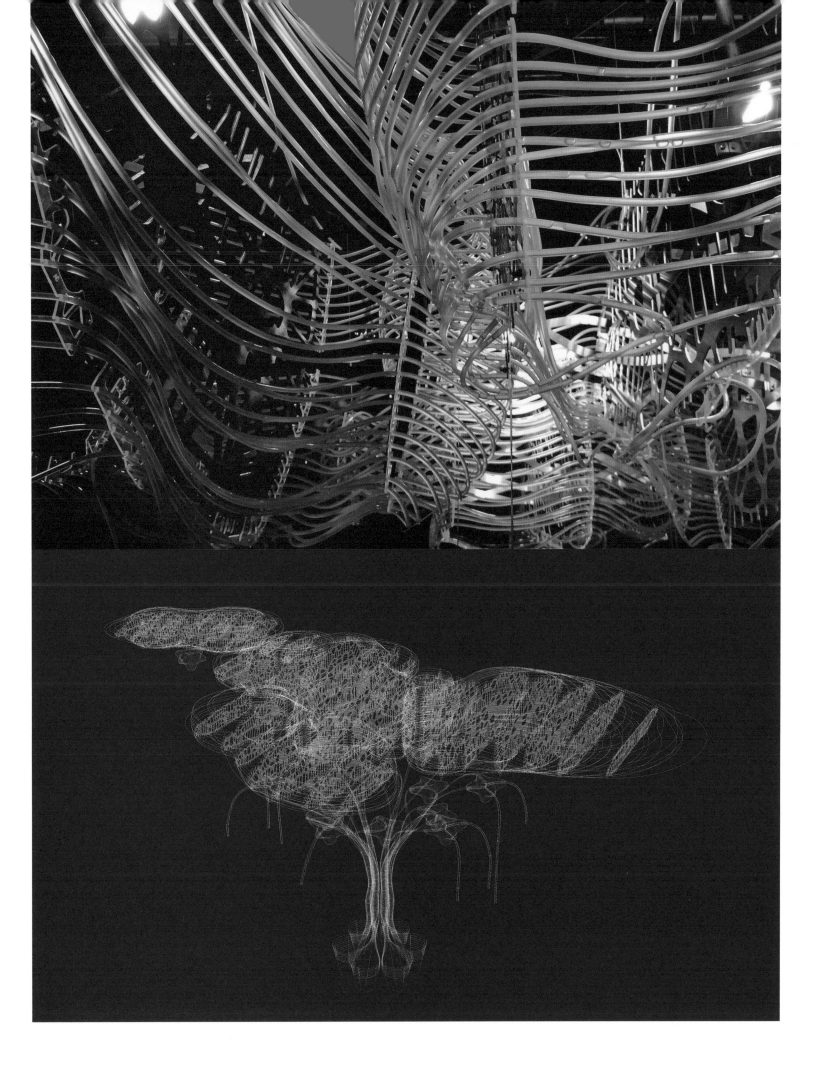

In research conducted with
Dr Sarah Eppley's laboratory at
Portland State University, Oregon,
Faulders explored the behaviour
of individual spores of fire moss –
notably, the patterns formed by the
moss as it matures, branches out and
replicates in search of nutrients and
light. Much more resistant to pollution
than other mosses, fire moss thrives
in urban and industrial environments,
making it ideal for Faulders's moss-
absorbing walls.

Bryophyte Building

Faulders Studio / Tehran, Iran

Thom Faulders, founder of Faulders Studio, prefers to design buildings as evolving organisms rather than static objects. Living skins appear in a number of his projects, from a garage façade in Miami, designed as a canvas for street art, to a façade concept for Dubai, in which sea water flowing through a tubular structure gradually adds layers of crystallized salt to the building's lace-like envelope. The Bryophyte Building (opposite), a proposal for Tehran, Iran, has its façades wrapped in a skin of moss. Capable of growing on stone and of completely covering both horizontal and vertical surfaces, moss becomes a key element in this ever-evolving design co-created with nature.

The air in Tehran, one of the world's most car-dependent yet verdant cities, 'is equally rich in aerosol plant spores and carbon fumes,' observes Faulders, as he explains how he used local conditions to design 'a building that wears what it absorbs from the air we breathe'. Hidden behind eight-storey-tall oriental planes, its south façade spends most of the time in shadow. Add irregular, highly 'clingable' surfaces and an integrated moisturizing system (that feeds on recycled water), and you have the perfect setting for attracting moss spores and fostering their growth. In addition to serving as an air purifier, this textured, velvety façade will dissipate and absorb the noise of street traffic.

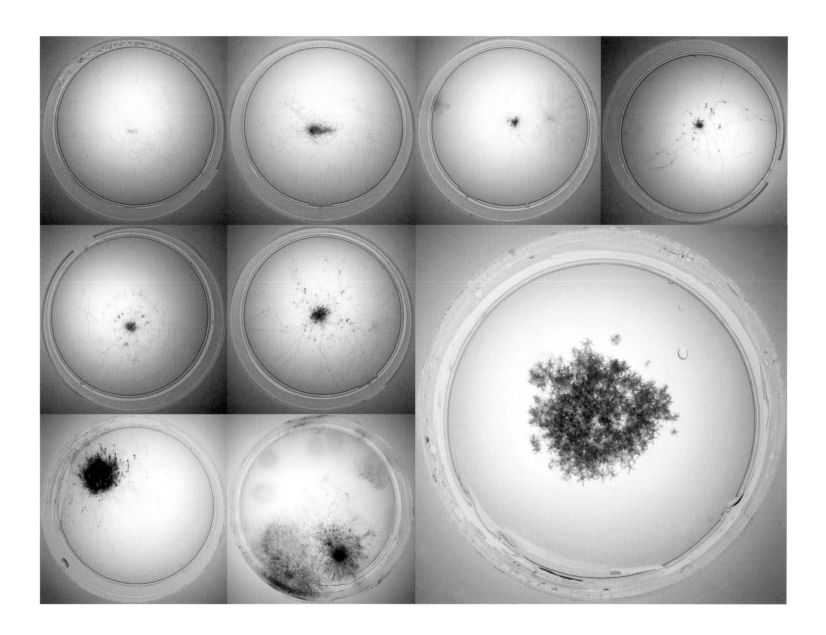

Hydrophile

Servo / Stockholm, Sweden

In their proposal for the Bioscience Innovation Centre in Sweden, Servo – an architectural firm with offices in Los Angeles and Stockholm – reconsidered the concept of a green roof to create what they call an 'occupiable roofscape', which can be experienced not only from above but also from below (in places where the roof nearly touches the floor) and from within – for instance, in the laboratories where plants will be cultivated in semi-controlled microclimates. Taking their cues from nature, the architects applied the water-attracting and water-repelling properties of the shell of the Namib Desert beetle to the design of the centre's hydrodynamic roof.

The use of ceramics with different levels of porosity and different surface treatments is coupled with variations in the roof's topography to provide suitable conditions for several communities of plants, from mosses and lichens that can survive in almost no amount of soil to those species that thrive in wet meadows and fens. The thickness of the soil substrates varies from less than 7 centimetres (2¾ inches) for drought-tolerant species to up to 35 centimetres (13¾ inches) for the wet areas. Various 'protuberances' in the roof help direct water towards a series of cavities, where it can be stored to support the wetland ecosystems. Planned for the edge of a national park, not far from Brunnsviken Bay, the new centre, complete with its cleverly integrated water system, will serve as a handsome pit stop for local amphibians.

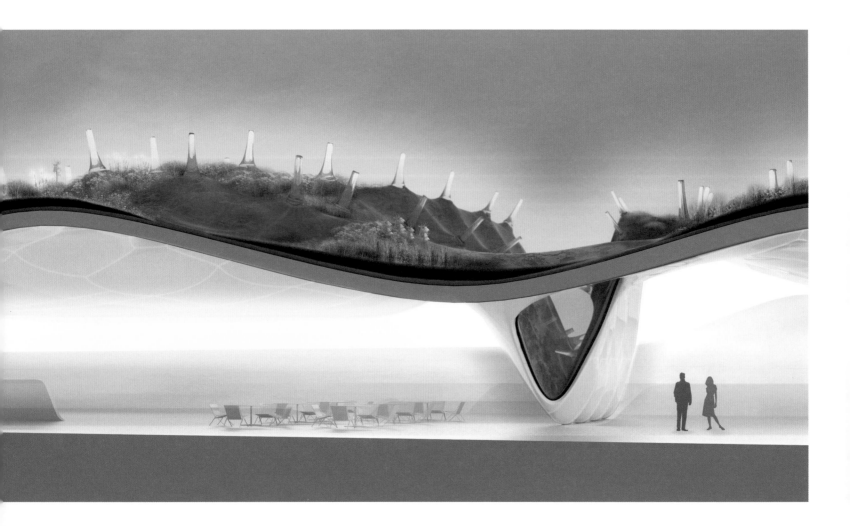

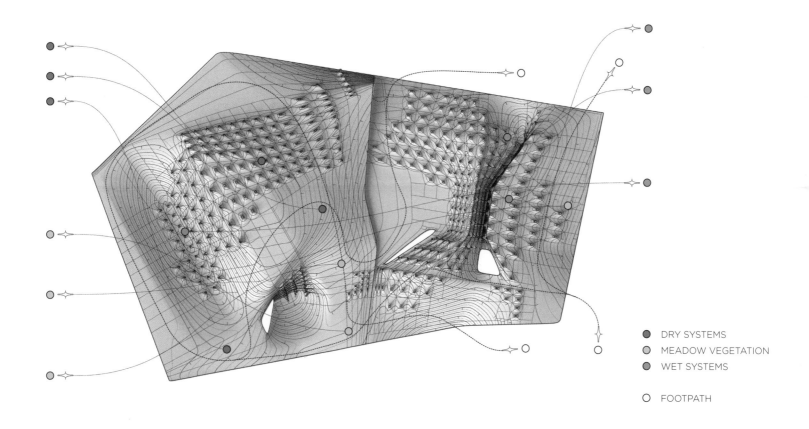

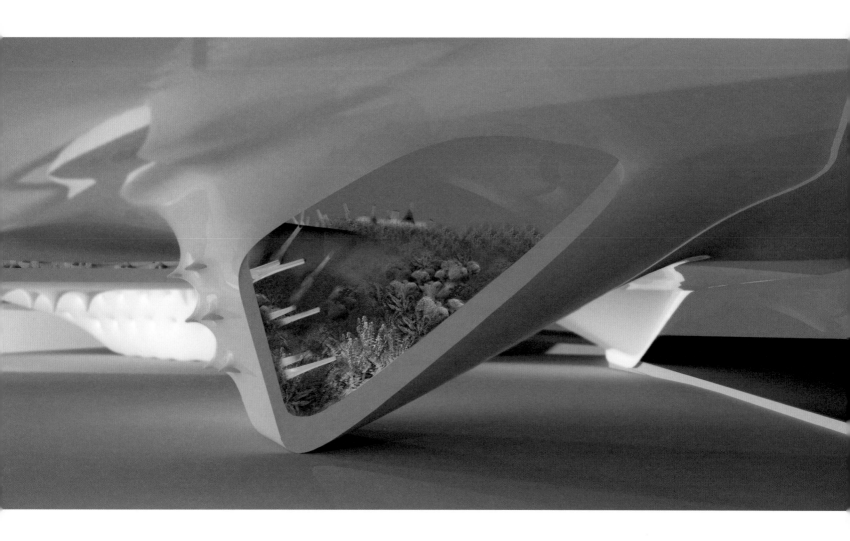

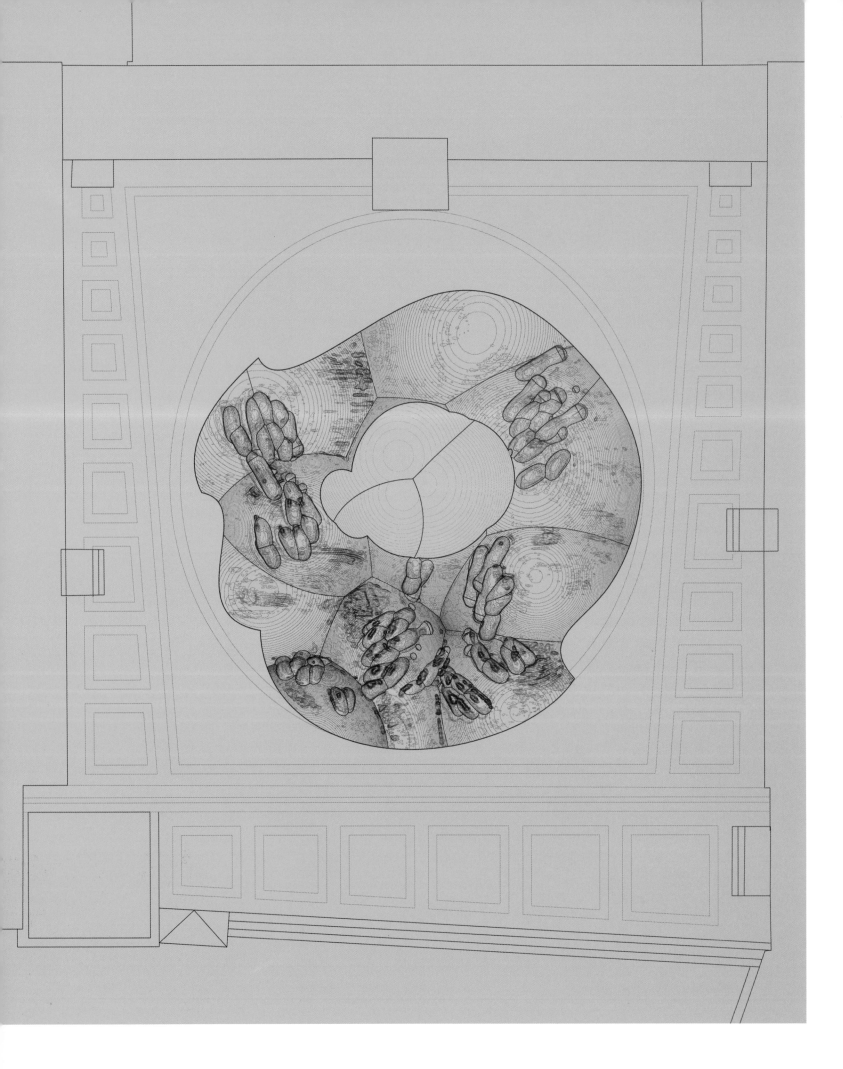

Vector Interference

Servo / Stockholm, Sweden

When Servo were asked to develop a proposal for a multipurpose, 500-square-metre (5,382-square-foot) facility at the KTH Royal Institute of Technology in Stockholm, they decided that their design should reflect the research and educational activities that would be taking place inside, thereby enabling the building's inner life to 'affect the built environment of the campus'. Led by Ulrika Karlsson and Marcelyn Gow of, respectively, Servo's Stockholm and Los Angeles offices, the design team used simple vector techniques to emulate a naturally eroded landform for the building's roof – complete with cavities and niches – as well as to enable the digital fabrication of such a complex topography. The roofscape will be planted with several kinds of drought-resistant mosses, but will also remain exposed in places, as if it were an actual moss-covered rock. A combination of water-repellent and water-absorbent surfaces will create dry and humid areas, thus boosting this micro-landscape's diversity.

breathe.austria

team.breathe.austria / Milan, Italy

An 'air-generating station' – a living, breathing forest packed inside a roofless pavilion – was the exhibit displayed by Austria at Expo 2015 in Milan, Italy. Responding to the Expo's theme, 'Feeding the Planet, Energy for Life', the multidisciplinary team led by Klaus Loenhart of Austrian–German design studio terrain: focused on air as an essential nutrient and one of our planet's most precious resources.

Called breathe.austria, and offering a much coveted escape from the sweltering Milanese summer, the pavilion was in fact a futuristic vision of nature and technology working in unison. In this augmented oasis, 190 species of mosses, grasses and trees drawn from twelve Austrian forest habitats were organized into a complex landscape in which such natural processes as cooling through water evaporation were enhanced by misting and ventilating machines. Pleasantly fresh without a single air conditioner, and generating enough oxygen per hour to satisfy the needs of 1,800 visitors, this hybrid forest was at the core of a meticulously engineered multisensory experience.

The team behind breathe.austria – architects, landscape designers and climate engineers – are convinced that similar combinations of natural and technological systems will cause a paradigm shift in the future. With an oxygen output equal to that of a natural forest fifty times the size of the pavilion, it was meant as an efficient and environmentally sound model for urban projects. Just imagine a network of such oases deployed in a city with high air-pollution rates.

The Austrian pavilion at Expo 2015 had a footprint of 560 square metres (6,028 square feet). High-pressure misting devices (opposite) installed in its walled forest were used to activate the entire evaporation surface of the plants – that is, about 43,200 square metres (465,000 square feet). As a result, the ambient temperature was lowered by some 5–7°C without the use of air conditioners, while the 62.5 kilograms (138 pounds) of oxygen per hour produced by this enhanced landscape equalled the output of a 3-hectare (7½-acre) forest. A photovoltaic system on the pavilion's roof and a sculpture composed of Grätzel solar cells ensured that the project self-generated all the electricity required for its functioning.

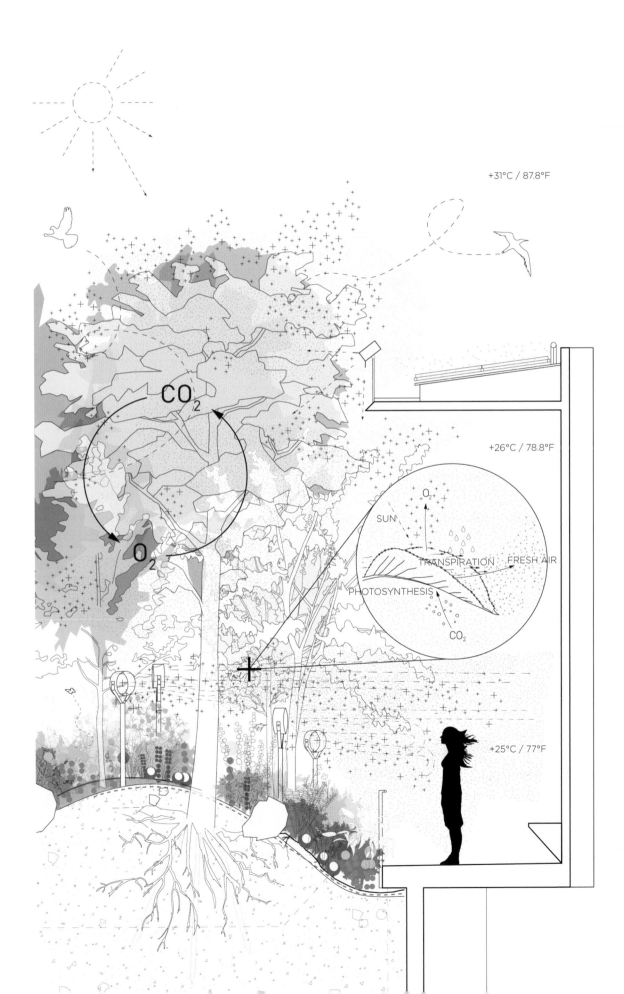

+31°C / 87.8°F

CO_2

O_2

+26°C / 78.8°F

O_2

SUN

TRANSPIRATION

FRESH AIR

PHOTOSYNTHESIS

CO_2

+25°C / 77°F

Jade Eco Park

Philippe Rahm Architectes, Mosbach Paysagistes, Ricky Liu & Associates / Taichung, Taiwan

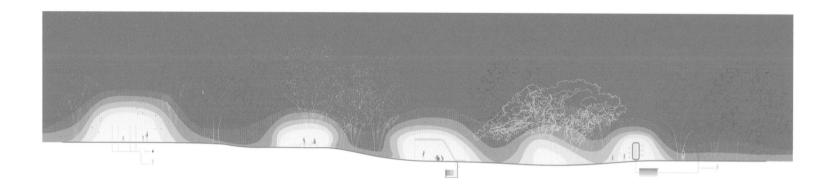

The benefits of marrying technology with the performance of nature itself are being explored on a more permanent basis in the 70-hectare (173-acre) Jade Eco Park. As architect Philippe Rahm, who has masterminded the whole experience, explains: 'Taichung is a big, polluted city with a hot and humid tropical climate. People spend a lot of time indoors, in air-conditioned spaces, getting disconnected from nature. This is why we decided to base the entire composition of the park on the idea of minimizing heat, humidity and pollution.'

With the help of CFD (computational fluid dynamics) software, the design team started by identifying the future park's coolest, driest and least polluted areas. Categorized, respectively, as a 'Coolia', 'Dryia' or 'Clearia' zone, the resulting eleven zones had their natural qualities amplified by a range of custom-built 'climatic devices'. Such devices, including mist machines, wind generators and systems capable of raising the air quality to that of pre-industrial levels, are powered by some

5,000 square metres (53,820 square feet) of solar panels. Landscape architect Catherine Mosbach provided the vegetal component of Rahm's carefully plotted climatic design. Her selection includes trees with cooling, dehumidifying and air-purifying properties, all strategically placed across the site.

The enormous park borders on different areas of the city and receives all kinds of visitors, from local residents and office employees to schoolchildren and tourists. The new park's ambition is to provide an extraordinary experience for each of them while enhancing their awareness of nature's workings. Every zone is fitted out for activities suited to its climate: relaxing pastimes, such as reading, web-surfing and chatting, in Coolia zones; sports and fitness in Dryia zones; and family leisure in Clearia zones. There is also a climate-change museum, whose exhibits include a replication of the meteorological conditions of 21 November, statistically Taiwan's driest day of the year.

The park is dotted with bespoke climatic devices that dry, cool or clean the atmosphere. Their functioning is based on natural phenomena.

The Cool Light, one of the devices designed for the park's Coolia zones, has a roof that incorporates a colour filter to block out light's warmer, longer waves.

The Anticyclone pumps air through a natural underground cooler to significantly reduce the outside temperature. The Cirrus Cloud (page 233, top) emits a cool mist that absorbs heat from the air as it evaporates. It also provides shade, just like an actual cirrus cloud.

Migrating Floating Gardens

Rael San Fratello

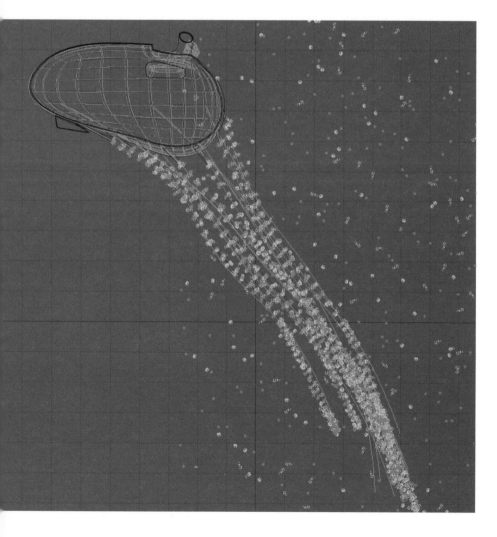

'Modernity and the development of dense, high-rise construction pushed green to rooftops to replace the area covered by the building on the ground,' say architects Ronald Rael and Virginia San Fratello. 'The current demand for "greener" cities has provoked architects to seek new sites where landscape can intervene in the city.' For the California-based duo, the next location for 'urban green' – after planted roofs and façades – is the sky.

The architects have imagined a series of floating gardens suspended from partly autonomous, partly remotely controlled dirigibles with photovoltaic skins. Integrated sensors would monitor weather, traffic, pollution, noise and other relevant data in real time, while propulsion devices would move the airborne gardens to where they were most needed, turning them into 'environmental ambulances'. A fleet of such dirigibles could soothe the 'heat island' effect seen above many cities, but could also migrate between cities and seasons, seeking the best climatic conditions to maintain plant life. By night, they would return to their home base in order 'to refuel, rehydrate and recalculate the data acquired'. The use of microbial fuel cells could turn these nomadic 'airscapes' into purifiers that consume water from contaminated rivers, decompose the pollutants and convert them into energy for propulsion.

A feasibility study would be no mean feat, requiring a multidisciplinary effort from robotics and horticulture experts, dirigible manufacturers, swarm-intelligence theorists and artificial-weather scientists, as well as, most probably, architects and landscape designers.

In Rael San Fratello's migrating garden concept, each dirigible would carry thousands of small epiphytic plants with attached sensors. 'Controlled by GPS and GIS information,' explain the architects, 'and organized in flocking patterns, plants [would] move through the city in swarms – hydrating, providing shade, increasing the local albedo and bringing oxygen to spaces devoid of green.'

Dragonfly

Vincent Callebaut Architectures / New York, NY

The design of this bionic tower takes its inspiration from the wings of a dragonfly. Extremely thin and lightweight, the transparent, finely veined membranes keep the use of material to a minimum. An ingenious combination of rigid and flexible areas provides the wings with a high level of performance, enabling them to carry the insect's much heavier body.

'What interests me about vertical farms', says architect Vincent Callebaut, 'is their potential for merging the twenty-first-century urban and rural models in a kind of metabolic architecture that generates heat, electric and nutritional energy.'

Designed in 2009, Callebaut's proposal for New York City's Roosevelt Island combines housing, offices, research laboratories and agricultural production in a building that is intended to function 24/7. Multistorey plantations are greenhoused between two fully glazed façades, which protect the plants from New York's varied climate while maximizing natural light. Offices and apartments are clustered inside the frame-like structure, which circumscribes the building's food-producing core. The two narrow façades produce electricity for this self-sufficient building: the prow-like south façade houses solar cells, while the north façade incorporates windmills to harvest the energy of the prevailing winds. Vertical gardens – which double as natural purifiers of the building's grey water – cover the two larger façades, with drought-tolerant plants selected for the Manhattan-facing side, and tropical species for the façade that overlooks Long Island City and benefits from a more humid atmosphere.

Rising Ryde

Architensions / Ryde, Australia

In their shortlisted design for the Ryde Civic Hub – a replacement for the ageing civic centre in a suburb of Sydney, Australia – Alessandro Orsini and Nick Roseboro from US-based firm Architensions refer to a 'vertical neighbourhood' rather than a complex of buildings.

The new hub combines community facilities with residential and commercial elements; a public square was an essential part of the brief. Indeed, this functional diversity is at the heart of Architensions's design. Based on the idea of 'architecture as a living system', in which 'micro-cells' are combined to achieve 'the macro scale of the city', it merges architecture with landscape by means of a transparent spatial grid with structural steel sections that support residential floors, circulation areas and green roofs. Social gathering spaces permeate the entire project: the team speaks of a large public plaza that extends from the ground up, in a sequence of vertical gardens and observation decks. Although the hub is surrounded by roads, 'soundscaping' makes it acoustically friendly. The entire mass is shaped to act as its own soundproofing screen, with residential parts moved away from the noisiest façade, while vegetation and water features provide natural sounds to mask unpleasant noises.

A set of site-specific environmental strategies was devised by climate engineers from Transsolar. Thus, the porous structure allows natural ventilation to cool the building, while a gravity-driven irrigation and rainwater-collection system enables stepped gardens with drought-tolerant plants to be self-sustaining.

Paris Smart City 2050

Vincent Callebaut Architectures / Paris, France

When he speaks of 'archibiotics', Vincent Callebaut means the merging of architecture, biology and information technologies to create hyper-connected cities that will function as natural ecosystems, with no pollution or waste. In a sense, he is looking to give architectural form to American economist and social theorist Jeremy Rifkin's concept of the Third Industrial Revolution – notably, Rifkin's ideas about transforming every building into a power plant and connecting them via a smart, peer-to-peer energy-sharing grid.

Challenged by Paris City Council to come up with ways of densifying the urban fabric while fulfilling the city's plan to reduce greenhouse-gas emissions by 75 per cent before 2050, Callebaut joined forces with experts in bioclimatic engineering from Setec to develop eight proposals for transforming Paris into a 'smart city'. But if you can't build one from scratch, as was the case with South Korea's Songdo or Abu Dhabi's Masdar, how *do* you create such a city?

The Photosynthesis Towers (opposite, top) will make use of the existing Montparnasse tower while adding two smaller ones, wrapping them in a verdant, piezoelectric spiral ramp. The result will be a fifty-eight-storey public park that will generate electricity from its visitors' footsteps. The new façades will incorporate photobioreactors for the production of microalgae as a source of biofuel.

The Bamboo Nest Towers (opposite, bottom) will envelop thirteen 1960s residential high-rises in a three-dimensional 'eco-skeleton' in plaited bamboo. The structure will support the load of vegetable-garden balconies, and use funnels to boost the output of wind turbines.

Convinced that treating the historic districts of Paris like museums would be detrimental to the city's future, Callebaut sought out evolutionary strategies that would be respectful of the past while resolutely open to new ideas. These include architectural extensions grafted on to existing buildings to create energy-efficient hybrids of old and new, '[mixing] nature and digital technologies to improve life quality in the increasingly saturated city'.

Callebaut's proposals explore historic, modern and completely futuristic ideas. Thus, the arcade buildings of the famous Rue de Rivoli (page 243) are complemented by so-called Mountain Towers that incorporate solar power systems into crystalline façades. The resulting energy is stored in a hydroelectric system that pumps water between two retention tanks, while 'garden balconies' produce food and reduce the 'heat island' effect.

The Farmscrapers (right, top and bottom) are intended for a new development area in northern Paris. Straddling the ring road, they will combine housing and farming in a stack of organic-shaped modules made possible by an innovative structural solution initially developed for a residential tower now under construction in Taipei, Taiwan.

The Mangrove Towers (opposite) emulate the structure of mangrove forests to reclaim the currently underused land within Paris's vast railway network. Their façades are clad with Grätzel solar cells, which convert the sun's energy into electricity by means of a process similar to photosynthesis.

X SEA TY & Fresh City

XTU Architects

These conceptual projects by XTU Architects envisage a symbiotic relationship between architecture, nature and technology as a solution to such city-related problems as high levels of pollution; agricultural land consumed by urban sprawl; and residents detached from nature. The practice of bringing nature into the city by 'greening' its façades inevitably raises maintenance issues. Making these façades productive, argue the architects, would justify maintenance costs.

Their X SEA TY (left and opposite, top) is a kind of 'offshore utopia' for a coastal Asian metropolis. Built over the water, this satellite city is composed of two kinds of buildings. The honeycomb façades of residential towers are made from growth-supporting concrete and act as major air purifiers. The curtain walls of office buildings incorporate photobioreactors, which use the abundant sunshine to grow microalgae.

Fresh City (opposite, below) is an alternative urban model for a 'difficult' site in south-eastern France, known for its hot climate and tendency to flood. Raised on stilts, the buildings avoid being flooded and leave the ground to flora and fauna. Façades are either made from air-purifying 'green concrete' or equipped with photobioreactors. The harvested biomass provides a source of fuel, thus ensuring the city's energy independence. As we have seen, XTU are now implementing some of these ideas – notably, biofaçades and green concrete – in real-life projects (pages 204–7 and 214–15).

List of Projects

List of Projects

Rising Ryde [241]
Architensions
Ryde, Australia

Ruin Academy Taitung [148]
Casagrande Laboratory
Taitung, Taiwan

Saigon House [136]
a21studio
Ho Chi Minh City, Vietnam

Shared Learning Centre [124]
Sou Fujimoto,
Manal Rachdi OXO Architects,
Laisné Roussel
Paris-Saclay, France

Siu Siu [116]
Divooe Zein
Taipei, Taiwan

Stacking Green [44]
Vo Trong Nghia Architects
Ho Chi Minh City, Vietnam

Stone Gardens [115]
Lina Ghotmeh – Architecture
Beirut, Lebanon

Stone House [32]
Vo Trong Nghia Architects
Dong Trieu, Vietnam

Sunken Garden [94]
Plasma Studio
Beijing, China

Third Landscape Gardens [93]
Coloco,
Gilles Clément
Saint-Nazaire, France

Torque House [54]
Mass Studies
Gyeonggi-do, South Korea

Tree Storey [38]
Penda
Vijayawada, India

Urban Algae Follies [216]
ecoLogicStudio

Vector Interference [227]
Servo
Stockholm, Sweden

Vertical Farms [194]
SOA Architectes

Vertical Forest [74]
Boeri Studio
Milan, Italy

Waterloo Youth Centre [24]
Collins and Turner
Sydney, Australia

White Walls – Tower 25 [12]
Jean Nouvel,
Takis Sophocleous Architects
Nicosia, Cyprus

X SEA TY [246]
XTU Architects

Project Credits

White Walls – Tower 25 [12]
Status: built (2015)
Programme: housng, offices, retail
Client: Nice Day Developments
Design architect: Ateliers Jean Nouvel
Collaborating architect: Takis Sophocleous
Architects
Structural engineers: KAL
Engineering: K. Lissandros

25 Green [15]
Status: built (2013)
Programme: housing
Client: Gruppo Corazza, Maina Costruzioni, DE-GA
Architect: Luciano Pia
Structural engineers: Giovanni Vercelli
Energy engineer: Andrea Cagni
Landscape consultants: Lineeverdi (Stefania
Naretto, Chiara Otella)
Contractor: DE-GA

House for Trees [18]
Status: built (2014)
Programme: single-family residence
Client: private
Architect: Vo Trong Nghia Architects
Contractor: Wind and Water House JSC

One Central Park [22]
Status: built (2014)
Programme: housing, retail
Client: Frasers Property Australia and Sekisui
House Australia
Design architect: Ateliers Jean Nouvel
Collaborating architect: PTW Architects
Landscape team: Ewen Le Ruic, Irene Djao-
Rakitine, Celine Aubernias
Structural engineers: Aedis (Davor Grgic)
Energy engineers: Transsolar (Matthias Schuler)
Green walls consultant: Patrick Blanc
Landscape consultant: Jean-Claude Hardy
Horizontal planters consultant: Aspect Oculus
Heliostat team: Kennovations (design);
Device Logic (programming); Yann Kersale
(lighting design)
Main contractor: Watpac Construction (NSW)

Waterloo Youth Centre [24]
Status: built (2012)
Programme: community services facility
Client: City of Sydney, Weave Youth Family
Community
Architect: Collins and Turner
Structural engineers: Arup
Environmental engineers: Team Catalyst
Landscape consultants: Terragram
Contractor: Projectcorp

House K [28]
Status: built (2012)
Programme: single-family residence
Client: private
Architect: Sou Fujimoto Architects
Structural engineers: Jun Sato, Kenichi Inoue
Landscape consultant: Furukawateijuen
(Motokazu Furukawa)
General contractor: Okuoka Koumuten

Stone House [32]
Status: built (2012)
Programme: single-family residence
Client: private (Mr Dinh Hoang Lien)
Architect: Vo Trong Nghia Architects
Contractor: Wind and Water House JSC

The Mountain [34]
Status: built (2007)
Programme: housing, parking garage
Client: Høpfner, Dansk Olie Kompagni
Architect: BIG – Bjarke Ingels Group
Collaborators: Plot, JDS, Moe & Brødsgaard

Tree Storey [38]
Status: ongoing
Programme: housing
Client: Pooja Crafted Homes
Architect: Penda Architecture & Design

Hualien Residences [42]
Status: ongoing (model home built: 2015)
Programme: housing estate
Client: TLDC – Taiwan Land Development
Corporation
Architect: BIG – Bjarke Ingels Group
Collaborators: RJ Wu, Arup

Stacking Green [44]
Status: built (2011)
Programme: single-family house
Client: private
Architect: Vo Trong Nghia Architects
Contractor: Wind and Water House JSC

The Building that Grows [46]
Status: built (2000)
Programme: housing
Client: Michel Troncin
Architects: Maison Édouard François; Duncan
Lewis – Scape Architecture
Structural engineers: Green & Hunt; Verdier
Contractor: Socamip

Biodiversity School [48]
Status: built (2014)
Programme: school complex, gymnasium
and recreational centre
Client: SAEM Val de Seine
Architect: Chartier Dalix Architectes
Structural engineers: EVP
HEQ (high environmental quality) engineers:
Franck Boutté
Ecology consultants: A.E.U.
Biodiversity consultants: Biodiversita
Contractor: Bouygues Ouvrages Publics

Chamber of Commerce and Industry of the Picardy Region [50]
Status: built (2012)
Programme: offices, auditorium and event space
Client: CRCI de Picardie
Architect: Chartier-Corbasson Architectes
Structural and mechanical engineers: BETOM
HEQ engineers: Cap Terre
Façade engineers: VSA

Torque House [54]
Status: built (2005)
Programme: single-family residence with studios
Client: private (Mr Doohyun Lee)
Architect: Mass Studies
Structural engineers: TEO Structure
Landscape consultant: Environmental Design
Studio
Contractor: Hanurim Construction

Ann Demeulemeester Store [56]
Status: built (2005)
Programme: retail
Client: Handsome Corp.
Architect: Mass Studies
Structural engineers: TEO Structure
Landscape consultants: Garden in Forest;
Vivaria Project
Contractor: Geomang Design

Flytower [61]
Status: completed (2007)
Programme: temporary public artwork
Commissioner: National Theatre
Artists: Ackroyd & Harvey

Cunningham [61]
Status: completed (2013)
Programme: temporary public artwork for
the Void Sites programme
Commissioner: Void
Artists: Ackroyd & Harvey

Project Credits

Diaspora Garden [68]
Status: built (2013)
Programme: thematic landscape sculpture
Client: Jewish Museum Berlin
Landscape architects: atelier le balto

FLEG Daikanyama [73]
Status: built (2005)
Programme: retail and offices
Client: FLEG International
Architect: Taketo Shimohigoshi/A.A.E.
Structural engineers: G.DeSIGN
General contractor: Nishimatsu Construction

Vertical Forest [74]
Status: built (2013)
Programme: housing
Client: Hines Italia
Architect: Boeri Studio
Aesthetic supervision: Francesco de Felice,
Davor Popovic
Structural engineers: Arup Italia
Vertical forest consultants: Emanuela Borio,
Laura Gatti
Landscape consultants: Land

Green Cloud/Panache [78]
Status: ongoing (scheduled completion: 2017)
Programme: housing
Client: Altarea Cogedim
Architect: Maison Édouard François
Collaborating architect: Aktis
Structural engineers: CTG

Green Cloud/Gurgaon 71 [78]
Status: ongoing
Programme: housing
Client: Krrish Group
Architect: Maison Édouard François

The Mile [81]
Status: concept proposal (2016)
Programme: entertainment and recreational
complex
Client: undisclosed
Architect: Carlo Ratti Associati
Collaborators: Schlaich Bergermann & Partner;
Atmos

The High Line [82]
Status: completed (three phases, 2009–14)
Programme: public park
Client: public–private partnership between the
City of New York and Friends of the High Line
Architect: Diller Scofidio + Renfro
Landscape architect and designer: James Corner
Field Operations (project lead); Piet Oudolf
Structural engineers: BuroHappold (structure
and MEP (mechanical, electrical, plumbing));
Robert Silman Associates (structural engineering
and historic preservation)

The Lowline [86]
Status: ongoing (scheduled opening: 2020)
Programme: public park
Architect: James Ramsey/RAAD Studio
Landscape consultants: Mathews Nielsen
Landscape architects: John Mini Distinctive
Landscapes; Brooklyn Botanic Garden
Rremote skylight systems: James Ramsey/
RAAD Studio (concept); Sunportal (engineering)

Asfalto Mon Amour [90]
Status: completed (2013–14)
Programme: workshops
Collaborators: Coloco; Labuat; LUA; Scuola del
Terzo Paesaggio

Third Landscape Gardens [93]
Status: completed (2009–11)
Programme: public landscaping artwork
Collaborators: Gilles Clément (concept); Coloco
(implementation)

Sunken Garden [94]
Status: built (2013)
Programme: exhibition garden
Client: Beijing Department of Construction
Management of the Horticultural Exposition
Architect: Plasma Studio
Collaborator: Groundlab

Croton Water Filtration Plant [96]
Status: ongoing
Programme: water-filtration facility, golf course
Client: New York City Department of
Environmental Protection
Architect: Grimshaw Architects
Landscape architect: Ken Smith Workshop
Engineers: Hazen Sawyer; Ammann & Whitney
Green roof consultants: Rana Creek
Ecology consultants: Great Ecology

The Foundry Garden [98]
Status: completed (2009)
Programme: public space
Client: Samoa
Architect, landscape designer:
Doazan+Hirschberger & Associés
Urban planners: BTP

MFO-Park [102]
Status: completed (2002)
Programme: public space
Client: Grün Stadt Zürich
General planner: Planergemeinschaft MFO-Park
burkhardtpartner/raderschall
Furniture design: Frédéric Dedeley

House Before House [110]
Status: built (2009)
Programme: model house for the Sumika Project
Client: Tokyo Gas
Architect: Sou Fujimoto Architects

Stone Gardens [115]
Status: ongoing
Programme: housing, offices and gallery space
Client: Fouad El Khoury, A&H, Red
Architect: Lina Ghotmeh – Architecture
(formerly DGT)
Local architect: Batimat

Siu Siu [116]
Status: built (2014)
Programme: showroom and event space
Client: Divooe Zein Architects
Architect: Divooe Zein Architects

Optical Glass House [120]
Status: built (2012)
Programme: single-family residence
Client: private
Architect: Hiroshi Nakamura & NAP
Structural engineer: Yasushi Moribe
Contractor: Imai Corporation

Shared Learning Centre [124]
Status: ongoing (scheduled completion: 2018)
Programme: learning centre
Client: École Polytechique Paris-Saclay
Architects: Sou Fujimoto Architects, Manal Rachdi
OXO Architects, Laisné Roussel
Engineers & HEQ consultants: Franck Boutté
Landscape consultants: MOZ Paysage
General contractor: Egis Bâtiments

House N [128]
Status: built (2008)
Programme: single-family residence
Client: private
Architect: Sou Fujimoto Architects
Structural engineer: Jun Sato

Bathyard Home [133]
Status: built (2008)
Programme: apartment refurbishment
Client: private
Architect: Husos Architects
Structural engineers: Mecanismo and
Eugenio Cuesta
Construction: Atipical (Daniel Jabonero)
and Husos (Camilo García)

Saigon House [136]
Status: built (2015)
Programme: single-family residence
Client: private (Ms Du)
Architect: a21studio
Contractor: 68 Construction

House in Moriyama [140]
Status: built (2009)
Programme: single-family residence
Client: private
Architect: Suppose Design Office

Cut Paw Paw [145]
Status: built (2014)
Programme: single-family residence
Client: private
Architect: Austin Maynard Architects
Engineers: Maurice Farrugia and Associates
Builder: Marc Projects

Ruin Academy Taitung [148]
Status: built (2014)
Programme: workshop, recreation and event
spaces in a disused industrial building
Commissioner: Taitung County Government
Architect: Casagrande Laboratory
Horticultural consultants: Mei-Hsiu Wang,
Ding-Yong Lin

Extreme Nature [152]
Status: completed (2008)
Programme: exhibition project
Commissioner: Taro Igarashi, curator of the
Japanese Pavilion at the Venice Biennale
Architect: Junya Ishigami+Associates
Structural engineer: Jun Sato
Landscape consultant: Hideaki Oba

House with Plants [154]
Status: built (2012)
Programme: single-family residence
Client: private
Architect: Junya Ishigami+Associates

Atelier Tenjinyama [158]
Status: built (2011)
Programme: office and residence
Client: private
Architect: Takashi Fujino – Ikimono Architects
Structural engineers: Akira Suzuki/ASA
Landscape consultants: ACID NATURE 0220
General contractor: Kenchikusha Shiki

Harmonia 57 [166]
Status: built (2008)
Programme: artists' residence
Client: private
Architect: Triptyque Architecture
Structural engineers: Rika (Rioske Kanno)
Hydraulics engineer: Guilherme Castanha
Landscape consultant: Peter Webb
Contractor: BGF; Aparecido Donizete Dias
Flausino

AMPS Wall [170]
Status: first application at the Public Safety
Answering Center II (2016)
Programme: Active Modular Phytoremediation
System for interior spaces
Developed by: Center for Architecture, Science
and Ecology (CASE) – Skidmore, Owings & Merrill
(SOM) and Rensselaer Polytechnic Institute

Drivhus [173]
Status: winning competition proposal
Programme: offices, conference hall, exhibition
space, rooftop café
Client: Stockholm City Council
Architects: SelgasCano; Urban Design
Landscape architect: Land Arkitektur
Structural, energy, HEQ consultants: Sweco

Eden Bio [175]
Status: built (2009)
Programme: social housing, artists' studios
Client: Paris Habitat
Architect: Maison Édouard François
Engineers: BETOM Ingénierie

Biodiversity Tower M6B2 [179]
Status: built (2016)
Programme: housing, daycare centre, retail
Client: Paris Habitat OPH
Architect: Maison Édouard François
Engineers: Arcoba (superstructure), Arcadis
(infrastructure)
Landscape consultants: BASE (landscape
designer); École du Breuil (vegetation
partnership)

Planted Tower of Nantes [179]
Status: competition proposal (2009)
Programme: housing, offices, retail
Client: Groupe OCDL Giboire
Architect: Maison Édouard François
Engineers: CERA Ingénierie

Host & Nectar Garden Building [182]
Status: built (phase 1: 2006; phase 2: 2012)
Programme: housing, textile manufacturing, retail
Client: Taller Croquis
Architect: Husos Architects, with the participation
of the local community
Structural consultants: Diego Gómez, Ángela
María Ramírez
Agronomy and entomology consultants:
Fundación Zoológico de Cali, Douglas Laing
(tropical agriculture engineering specialist),
Lorena Ramírez (biologist, University of Valle),
Luis M. Constantino (biologist, entomologist,
Associate Researcher at the National Centre for
Investigations in Coffee Cenicafé), Ricardo A.
Claro (biologist, entomologist, National University
of Colombia), José Martín Cano (biologist,
entomologist, Autonomous University of Madrid),
María García, Manuel Salinas, Julián Velásquez

Réalimenter Masséna [186]
Status: winning competition proposal (scheduled
completion: 2018)
Programme: urban farming, housing, offices,
workshop, retail, concert and exhibition spaces
Investor developer: Hertel
Architect: Lina Ghotmeh – Architecture
(formerly DGT)
Operators: ADC + VIRGIL (community
participation); AgroParisTech (research and
development); Alimentation Générale (cultural
operator); Engie Ineo (technological innovation);
La Ruche qui dit Oui (market, workshops);
Magda Danysz Gallery (street art gallery); NQ13
(neighourhood association); Polychrone (cultural
operator); Sous les Fraises (urban farming)
Structural and façade engineers: Bollinger +
Grohmann
HEQ consultants: Elan Environnement

Project Credits

Pasona HQ [190]
Status: built (2010)
Programme: offices, urban farming
Client: Pasona Group
Architect: Kono Designs
Structural engineers: Kajima Corporation
Landscape and farm consultants: Green Wise
General contractor: Taisei Corporation (exterior),
Nomura (interior)

Vertical Farms [194]
Status: prospective research studies (2005–12)
Programme: case studies and critical analysis for
farming in dense urban environments
Architect: SOA Architectes

Market Garden Tower [198]
Status: winning competition proposal (scheduled
completion: 2018)
Programme: urban vertical greenhouse
Client: OPH Romainville Habitat
Architect: Ilimelgo, Secousses
Structural engineers: Scoping
HEQ engineers: Etamine
Agronomy consultants: Terr'eau Ciel
Landscape consultants: Land'Act

Plantagon [201]
Status: ongoing
Programme: urban industrial vertical greenhouse
Client: Plantagon International
Architect: Sweco

Biofaçade (In Vivo) [204]
Status: winning competition proposal
Programme: housing, microalgae farming, retail,
workshop spaces
Client: BPD Marignan, Groupe SNI
Architect: XTU Architects, MU Architecture
Biofaçade development: SymBIO2
Engineering consultants: ATEC Ingénierie
HEQ consultants: OASIIS
Collaborators: Centre Michel Serres
(interdisciplinary innovation); Collectif Babylone
(urban farming); Groupe AlgoSource (microalgae
production and processing); Le Mur (urban art);
Mon P'ti Voisinage (local social networking);
Pharm'Alg (microalgae-based medical research);
La Paillasse (research lab)

Rising Canes [212]
Status: concept and prototype (ongoing)
Function: structural system
Developed by: Penda Architecture & Design

Green Concrete [215]
Status: product
Function: construction material
Developed by: XTU Architects

Urban Algae Follies [216]
Status: prototype, pavilion, sculpture (ongoing)
Programme: integrated urban facilities for
microalgae production
Architect: ecoLogicStudio
Partner at EXPO 2015: Carlo Ratti Associati
Digital responsive systems: Alt N – Nick Puckett
Structural engineers: Mario Segreto, Nicola Morda
(EXPO 2015); Format Engineers (Braga)
ETFE contractor: Taiyo Europe

H.O.R.T.U.S. [220]
Status: installation, bio-digital sculpture (ongoing)
Programme: light-responsive bio-digital sculpture
Developed by: ecoLogicStudio

Bryophyte Building [223]
Status: concept proposal (2009-13)
Programme: moss-based air-purifying façade
Architect: Faulders Studio
Collaborator: Eppley Laboratory; Portland State
University, OR

Hydrophile [224]
Status: concept proposal (2010)
Programme: bioscience innovation centre with
a hydrodynamic vegetated roof
Funding: Swedish Research Council
Architects: Servo Los Angeles, Servo Stockholm
Green roof and ecological consultant: Tobias
Emilsson
Collaborators: KTH School of Architecture,
Hanna Erixon, Lars Marcus, William Mohline,
Jonah Fritzell

Vector Interference [227]
Status: concept proposal (2014)
Programme: multipurpose learning centre
Client: KTH Royal Institute of Technology
Architect: Servo Stockholm, Servo Los Angeles,
KTH School of Architecture – Architecture Design
Research Group
Structural engineer: Oliver Tessmann
Energy systems: KTH ABE Civil and Architectural
Engineering
Forest raw materials consultant: Innventia
Green roof and ecology consultant: Tobias
Emilsson

breathe.austria [228]
Status: built (2015)
Programme: exhibition pavilion
Client: Federal Ministry of Science, Research and
Economy, Austria/The Austrian Federal Economic
Chamber
General planner: terrain: architects and landscape
architects BDA
team.breathe.austria: terrain: architects and
landscape architects BDA – Klaus K. Loenhart

in cooperation with Agency in Biosphere –
Markus Jeschaunig; Hohensinn Architektur ZT
GmbH – Karlheinz Boiger; LANDLAB; i_a&l;
TU-Graz – Andreas Goritschnig and Bernhard
König; Lendlabor Graz – Anna Resch and Lisa
Enzenhofer and Alexander Kellas; Engelmann
Peters Engineers – Stefan Peters; transsolar –
Wolfgang Kessling; BOKU Wien IBLB – Bernhard
Scharf; Büro Auinger – Sam Auinger

Jade Eco Park [232]
Status: completed (2017)
Programme: public park with recreational spaces,
climatic installations, museum
Client: Taichung City Government
Architect: Philippe Rahm Architectes
Local architect: Ricky Liu & Associates
Landscape architect: Mosbach Paysagistes

Migrating Floating Gardens [236]
Status: concept proposal (2007)
Programme: mobile green spaces with climate-
controlling and -purifying functions
Architect: Rael San Fratello

Dragonfly [238]
Status: concept proposal (2009)
Programme: housing, offices, urban farm
Architect: Vincent Callebaut Architectures

Rising Ryde [241]
Status: second-stage shortlisted competition
proposal (2016)
Programme: civic hub, housing, commercial, and
outdoor public spaces
Architect: Architensions
Climate engineering: Transsolar
Structural engineering: Format

Paris Smart City 2050 [242]
Status: prospective research studies (2014-15)
Programme: eight prototypes of positive-energy
towers based on historical, modern and new
construction
Client: Paris City Hall
Architect: Vincent Callebaut Architectures
Sustainable engineering: Setec

X SEA TY [246]
Status: concept proposal (2010)
Programme: sustainable urban-development plan
for large harbour cities
Architect: XTU Architects

Fresh City [246]
Status: concept proposal (2010)
Programme: sustainable urban-development plan
for an area with challenging climatic conditions
Architect: XTU Architects

Design Directory:
Architects, Landscape Architects and Artists

a21 studio [136]
a21studio.com.vn / Ho Chi Minh City, Vietnam
A.A.E./Taketo Shimohigoshi [73]
aae.jp / Tokyo, Japan
Ackroyd & Harvey [61]
ackroydandharvey.com / Dorking, Surrey, UK
Architensions [241]
architensions.com / Brooklyn, NY
atelier le balto [68]
lebalto.de / Berlin, Germany
Ateliers Jean Nouvel [12, 22]
jeannouvel.com / Paris, France
Atmos [81]
atmosstudio.com / London, UK
Austin Maynard Architects [145]
maynardarchitects.com / Melbourne, Australia
Base [179]
baseland.fr / Paris, Lyon and Bordeaux, France
BIG – Bjarke Ingels Grou [34, 42]
big.dk / Valby, Denmark, and New York City, NY
Boeri Studio [74]
stefanoboeriarchitetti.net / Milan, Italy
Burkhardt+Partner [102]
burckhardtpartner.ch / Basel, Switzerland
Carlo Ratti Associatir [81]
carloratti.com / Turin, Italy
Casagrande Laboratory [148]
casagrandelaboratory.com / Helsinki, Finland
Chartier-Corbasson Architectes [50]
chartcorb.free.fr / Paris, France
Chartier Dalix Architectes [48]
chartier-dalix.com / Paris, France
Collins and Turner [24]
collinsandturner.com / Surry Hills, Sydney,
Australia
Coloco [90, 93]
coloco.org / Paris, France
Diller Scofidio + Renfro [82]
dsrny.com / New York City, NY
Divooe Zein Architects [116]
divooe.com.tw / Taipei City, Taiwan
Doazan+Hirschberger & Associates [98]
doazan-hirschberger.com / Bordeaux, France
ecoLogicStudio [216, 220]
ecologicstudio.com / London, UK
Faulders Studio [223]
faulders-studio.com / Oakland, CA
Grimshaw Architects [96]
grimshaw-architects.com / New York City, NY;
London, UK; Doha, Qatar;
Melbourne and Sydney, Australia
Hiroshi Nakamura & NAP Architects [120]
nakam.info / Tokyo, Japan

Hohensinn Architektur [228]
hohensinn-architektur.at / Graz, Austria
Husos Architects [133, 182]
husos.info / Madrid, Spain
Ilimelgo Architectes [198]
ilimelgo.com / Paris, France
James Corner Field Operations [82]
fieldoperations.net / New York City, NY
John Mini Distinctive Landscapes [86]
johnmini.com / Congers, NY
Junya Ishigami & Associates [152, 154]
jnyi.jp / Tokyo, Japan
Ken Smith Workshop [96]
kensmithworkshop.com / New York City, NY
Kono Designs [190]
konodesigns.com / New York City, NY
Laisné Roussel [124]
laisneroussel.com / Montreuil, France
Land'Act [198]
land-act.fr / Levallois-Perret, France
Land Arkitektur [173]
landarkitektur.se / Stockholm, Sweden
Lendlabor [228]
lendlabor.at / Graz, Austria
Lina Ghotmeh – Architecture [115, 186]
linaghotmeh.com / Paris, France
Luciano Pia [15]
lucianopia.it / Turin, Italy
Maison Édouard François [46, 78, 175, 179]
edouardfrancois.com / Paris, France
Manal Rachdi OXO Architectes [124]
oxoarch.com / Paris, France
Mass Studies [54, 56]
massstudies.com / Seoul, Korea
Mathews Nielsen Landscape Architects [86]
mnlandscape.com / New York City, NY
Mosbach Paysagistes [232]
mosbach.fr / Paris, France
MOZ Paysage [124]
mozpaysage.com / Lyon, France
MU Architecture [204]
mu-architecture.fr / Paris and Tours, France
Penda Architecture & Design [38, 212]
home-of-penda.com / Beijing, China
Philippe Rahm Architectes [232]
philipperahm.com / Paris, France
Piet Oudolf [82]
oudolf.com / Hummelo, Netherlands
Plantagon [201]
plantagon.com / Stockholm, Sweden;
Shanghai, China; Mumbai, India, and Singapore
Plasma Studio [94]
plasmastudio.com / London, UK;

Beijing and Hong Kong, China, and Bolzano, Italy
PTW Architects [22]
ptw.com.au / Sydney, Australia;
Beijing, Shanghai and Shenzhen, China;
Ho Chi Minh City and Hanoi, Vietnam,
and Taipei City, Taiwan
Raad Studio [86]
raadstudio.com | New York City, NY
Raderschall Partner [102]
raderschall.ch | Melien, Switzerland
Rael San Fratello [236]
rael-sanfratello.com | Oakland, CA
Ricky Liu & Associates [232]
rickyliu.com.tw / Taipei City, Taiwan
Secousses [198]
secousses.com / Paris, France
SelgasCano [173]
selgascano.net / Madrid, Spain
Servo [224, 227]
servo-la.com, servo-stockholm.com
Los Angeles, CA and Stockholm, Sweden
SOA Architectes [194]
soa-architectes.fr / Paris, France
SOM – Skidmore, Owings & Merrill [170]
som.com / New York City, NY; Chicago, IL;
San Francisco and Los Angeles, CA;
Washington, DC; London, UK;
Hong Kong and Shanghai, China
Sou Fujimoto Architects [28, 110, 124, 128]
sou-fujimoto.net / Tokyo, Japan
Suppose Design Office [140]
suppose.jp / Hiroshima, Japan
Sweco [173, 201]
sweco.se / Stockholm, Sweden
Takashi Fujino/Ikimono Architects [158]
sites.google.com/site/ikimonokenchiku/home
Takasaki, Japan
Takis Sophocleous Architects [12]
sophocleous.net / Larnaka, Cyprus
Terragram [24]
terragram.com.au / Surry Hills, Sydney, Australia
terrain: [228]
terrain.de / Graz, Austria Munich, Germany
Triptyque Architecture [166]
triptyque.com / Sao Paolo, Brazil, and Paris, France
Urban Design [173]
urbandesign.se / Stockholm, Sweden
Vincent Callebaut Architectures [238, 242]
vincent.callebaut.org / Paris, France
Vo Trong Nghia Architects [18, 32, 44]
votrongnghia.com / Ho Chi Minh City, Vietnam
XTU Architects [204, 215, 246]
x-tu.com / Paris, France

Picture Credits

Anna Yudina is an author and curator primarily interested in the overlap between architecture, design, art, science and technology. She was a co-founder of *Monitor* magazine, which focused on innovations in contemporary architecture and design. She has been the curator of a number of international architecture and design exhibitions, including shows on Zaha Hadid and Jakob + MacFarlane, and is the author of *Furnitecture* and *Lumitecture*, also published by Thames & Hudson.

All drawings, diagrams and other illustrations are provided courtesy of the architect, unless otherwise specified.

2, **18-21**, **32-3**, **44-5** (photos) Hiroyuki Oki; **8-9**, **50-3** Yves Marchand & Romain Meffre; **12-13** Yiorgis Yerolymbos, courtesy of Nice Day Developments; **14-17** Beppe Giardino; **22-3** Roland Halbe; **24** (left) Paul Bradshaw; **24-5**, **26-7** (photo) Richard Glover; **28-9**, **30-1** (photo), **34-5**, **128-31** (photos) Iwan Baan; **36** Jakob Boserup; **37** Jens Lindhe; **43** (photo) Jinho Lee; **46** Paul Raftery; **47** (top) Nicolas Borel, (bottom) Édouard François; **49** (top right) David Foessel, (bottom) Philippe Guignard, courtesy of SAEM Val de Seine Aménagement; **54-9** (photos) Yong-Kwan Kim; **64-5**, **98-101** Hervé Abbadie; **68-71** hiepler, brunier; **72** Koichi Torimura; **73**, **112-13** (photo) Shigeo Ogawa; **74-7** Paolo Rosselli; **79** Luxigon; **82** Courtesy Friends of the High Line; **83-5** Troy Khasiev; **86-7** Cameron R Neilson; **89** (bottom) Philip Lange; **91** Danilo Capasso; **92** Pierre Couy-Perrais; **93** (top) Julie Guiches; **95** (top) Holger Kehne; **96-7** Alex MacLean; **102-5** Planergemeinschaft MFO-Park burkhardtpartner/raderschall; **110-11** Daici Ano; **120-3** (photos) Koji Fujii/Nacasa & Partners Inc.; **124-7** RSI-studio, Manal Rachdi OXO Architects, Laisné Roussel; **132-5** (photos) Miguel de Guzman + Rocio Romero/Imagen Subliminal; **136-9** (photos) Quang Tran; **140-3** (photos) Toshiyuki Yano/Nacasa & Partners Inc.; **144-6**, **147** (bottom) Peter Bennetts; **147** (top) Austin Maynard Architects; **148-51** (photos) AdDa Zei; **162-3**, **204-6**, **214-15**, **246-7** XTU Architects; **166-7** Leonardo Finotti; **167** (right), **168** (top right) Nelson Kon; **168** (top left), **169**, **248** Ricardo Bassetti; **170** © CASE | Rensselaer; **171** (bottom and top left) courtesy SOM/© CASE; **171** (top right) © CASE | Rensselaer | SOM; **174**, **177** Axel Dahl; **175**, **176** (right) David Boureau; **176** (left) Nicolas Castet; **178**, **180** Pierre L'Excellent; **182-3** Pedro Ruiz; **184**, **185** (top) Manuel Salinas; **191-3** Luca Vignelli; **200-3** © Plantagon. Illustration: Sweco; **207** Paul Desmazieres; **223** courtesy of Eppley Laboratory and Faulders Studio; **228-9** Marc Lins; **230** press@terrain; **231** team.breathe.austria; **240-1** Architensions